ANGELS

DAVE WILLIAMS

Angels

They Are Watching You!

DAVE WILLIAMS

Angels
They Are Watching You!

ISBN 0-938020-66-8

First Printing 2002

Published by

DECAPOLIS
PUBLISHING
Printed in the United States of America

BOOKS BY DAVE WILLIAMS

Contents

Foreword by Ken Gaub

How do angels fly? They take themselves lightly.

Okay...seriously now.

It seems that everywhere you look today you see "angels." There are web pages dedicated to the topic of angels, television programs, books, movies, figurines, cards, statues, and even angel fan clubs. Much of this may be innocent in nature, yet it could lead to a major deception if it's not lined up with God's Word. That is what Dave Williams does for you throughout this book. He lines up angel experiences with God's Word.

Angels *are* real. I know this is true from studying God's Word for more than forty years, and I know it's true from personal experiences with angels that harmonized with Bible accounts. Yes, I believe in angels. They have helped me on several occasions in response to my prayers to God. In chapter eleven, Pastor Dave Williams shares one of these marvelous experiences.

I'm always on the go; I travel all over with our world wide ministry. I need the help of God's ministering spirits to accomplish all He has called me to accomplish. Whether I'm taking supplies into war-torn regions of the world, taking a group of people to Israel, or ministering here in the U.S., I need angelic help.

God is good — very good! He sends angels to help even when we may not realize it. So what do you do when you meet an angel? Chapter fourteen will give you some quick guidelines. What about UFOs? That gets covered in chapter seven.

Dave Williams is my friend. He writes in a simple, easy to understand format. As you read *Angels — They are Watching You*, you'll sense a warmth and sincerity that will touch your heart. You'll be encouraged if you are facing a fearful or agonizing situation. The Holy Spirit will speak to you through this book. Be open. Be ready. Prepare for a miracle in your life.

You can read this book in just a couple of hours. My guess is that you won't be able to put it down once you start to read. You are about to have a close encounter of the supernatural kind, so sit down, relax, and let's take a journey into the realm of the invisible world and find out some surprising things about these mysterious creatures called angels. And remember, they are watching you...right now.

Ken Gaub
Ken Gaub World Wide Ministries
Yakima, WA, USA

We were meant to co-exist with angels, appreciating what they do, and respecting their place in God's creation.

First Thoughts

Something about angels attracts us, fascinates us, and makes us wonder. According to a major magazine, nearly seventy percent of Americans believe in angels. That is more than the number of Americans who consider themselves to be born again, and far more than the number of Americans who regularly attend church.

Angels represent a kind of safe religion. In the past few decades, people have begun to look to angels for hope, guidance and strength. Angels represent a spiritual yearning, a wishfulness for that other world we know is just beyond our senses.

Some people think angels will be whatever we want them to be. Some people think they are other worldly beings who drop in to help us now and then. Some people think they are evolved humans, or alien beings from another planet.

Men and women throughout history have wondered about angels — this other order of beings that God created.

- Where do they come from?

- What is their purpose?

- How are they different from mankind?

- Should we communicate with them?

- Are they higher or lower than us in God's scale of creation?

- Should we desire to see them?

- How do we tell a good angel from a bad one?

There are dozens and perhaps hundreds of books about angels in bookstores, so why the need for another one? Because even though people are open to angels and spirituality, they do not always receive teaching that is sound, truthful or safe. There is a persistent need for books that draw conclusions based entirely and solely on the Bible, and that is what I do in this book. The purpose is to clearly state who angels are, what their purpose is, and how we should relate to them. In the course of this book we will answer all of the questions listed above.

These pages are full of stories about angels, how they have interacted with people in Bible days and in our own day. The research and truths found in this book will add to your knowledge and wonder of angels, and all within the boundaries of what the Bible says. In fact, one of my goals is to establish clear boundaries so that Christians can find a healthy balance between ignoring the presence of angels — which is a non-biblical attitude — and seeking angels instead of God, which is also non-biblical.

We were meant to co-exist with angels, appreciating what they do, respecting their place in God's creation, working with them to bring God's plan to fruition. But it is wise to remember that God is our ultimate resource and authority, and that angels are His servants. Without God there are no angels, no earth, no you and me. It is Him we serve, and we should let our fascinations ultimately rest on the Creator, not anything He has created.

Let's look into this subject of angels to learn more about God, about ourselves and about our purpose on this planet. When we are through, you will be wonderfully enlightened about angels and have a greater appreciation for what God has empowered them to do.

Dave Williams

St. Petersburg, Florida

If we could lift the veil of the spirit realm, we would see angels everywhere.

Chapter 1

Close Encounters

Have you ever seen an angel? Dreamed of angels? Felt an angel nearby?

Do you know somebody who says he or she saw an angel? Do you believe it?

Have you ever wished you could see an angel? Have there been times when you wanted one to swoop out of the heavens and deliver you from a bad situation, such as a traffic jam or a fight with a loved one?

Have you ever been alone somewhere, maybe taking a walk or at home reading a book, and wondered if you were really alone? Have you pondered the idea that angels might be watching you as you go through your day?

I think most of us have had these thoughts. Our senses may tell us that we are alone, but in our spirits we have a deeper sense that we are not.

In fact, the Bible tells us we are not alone. As Christians, God is with us all the time. Jesus said:

> **I will not leave you as orphans; I will come to you.**
>
> —John 14:18

But God is not the only one with us from that invisible realm. He also sends angels to help us and carry out His will. If you are sitting in what appears to be an empty room, it is not really empty. When you drive down the highway you are not alone. That feeling you have of being with someone else is true: God is with you, and so are His angels.

Angels are closer to us than most people think. They are on divine commissions to carry out some purpose, some task. The Bible calls them "watchers" (Daniel 4:13 KJV). They are watching you right now. They watch you at home, at work, at school, in the pew at church. If we could lift the veil of the spirit realm, we would see angels everywhere.

Do I believe in angels? Yes, even though some theologians say that angels are nothing more than inspirations, sweet motivations, holographic wisps, or metaphors for the feeling of God's presence. I believe angels have personalities, and are created beings that are real and alive and in our midst. I know this to be true because that is the picture of angels the Bible gives us.

Not only do I believe in angels, I am excited about angels! Who wouldn't be thrilled to know we have supernatural partners in this work to which God has called us? Who doesn't want to be protected, helped, motivated, and provided for by heavenly beings?

Angels Through History

Famous people have had encounters with angels. George Washington claimed an angel visited him one day and showed him three wars the United States would face.

George Handel, when he was composing *The Messiah*, came out of a writing session and his face was radiant and wet with tears. He said angels were all around the room and he could take no credit for composing that masterpiece because angels from Heaven had given it to him. Even today, his music still rings with divine inspiration.

Billy Graham wrote a book called *Angels, God's Secret Agents*. Since that time, the aging evangelist has had his share of physical struggles. One time, in frustration, he announced that he was ready to retire and go to Heaven. Have you ever had one of those days where you wanted to pull the covers over your head and say, "God, I want out of here. Heaven is so much better than this place."

But an angel came to Billy and said, "You are not going to go Home until your work is done. You have to keep preaching." As of this writing, Billy is a very frail man until he gets into the pulpit and the power of God comes on him and he preaches with more anointing than ever. Just a few years ago he was ready to retire and go to be with Jesus, but he keeps going because an angel from God told him to keep preaching the Gospel.

Thirty years ago, if you said you believed in angels, you were considered weird. People back then believed in progress, hard work, the American way — but not angels.

That has changed. Today, references to angels are everywhere. There is music about angels, books about angels, angel web sites, angel newsletters, angel 900 numbers. Tour companies actually offer tour packages to angel conferences!

In the 1950s there were just a handful of movies about angels, the most popular being *It's a Wonderful Life* with Jimmy Stewart. Who can forget Clarence the angel who is trying earn his wings by helping George Bailey realize that life is worth living?

Today angel movies abound. There is *City of Angels, Ghost, Michael, Angels in the Outfield, Heaven Can Wait,* and television programs like *Touched by An Angel.*

This resurgence of interest in angels comes with a new interest in spiritual things of all kinds. Scan the television listings to see programs like *The X-Files, Unsolved Mysteries* and *Sightings.* They delve into supernatural, weird, mysterious things. They like to dwell on ghosts, aliens, conspiracies, and death. Other shows like *It's a Miracle,* and *Twice in a Lifetime* offer more positive views of the supernatural world.

You can't go into a card shop anymore without seeing angel displays. There are bumper stickers that say, "Angels are watching over me." People put angels on their dashboards, on their refrigerators, on their bathroom mirrors.

It seems that the spiritual world is en vogue. Even in the world of science it is not taboo to express belief in another world coexisting with the physical universe. Scientists, though they cannot quantify it, are coming to understand the reality of spiritual things. The spirit world may be made of a substance that is different than matter. In fact, scientists have discovered another world made from a substance that we cannot see called "anti-matter." Perhaps in all of their questioning and testing they have bumped up against the realm of Heaven and angels.

Angels In The Church

If anyone should know about angels, it should be Christians. The early church, Paul particularly, took for granted that angels were watching.

> For it seems to me that God has put us apostles on display at the end of the procession, like men condemned to die in the arena. We have been made a spectacle to the whole universe, *to angels* as well as to men.
>
> —1 Corinthians 4:9 (italics added)

> I charge you, in the sight of God and Christ Jesus *and the elect angels*, to keep these instructions without partiality, and to do nothing out of favoritism.
>
> —1 Timothy 5:21 (italics added)

Clearly, Paul believed that angels observe the goings-on of humanity. But somehow the Church got away from a balanced approach toward angels. At times throughout history, especially in the middle ages, there was a great deal of emphasis on angelic interventions and supernatural activity that did not always line up with the Word of God.

But until recently it seems the Church swung the other way. I clearly remember a time when believing in the active participation of angels meant you were a strange Christian, and maybe even a heretic. In the 1950s, believing that angels were our partners meant you were a holy roller, went to church on the wrong side of the tracks, and were not accepted in mainstream Protestant Christianity.

In traditional churches back then, you did not hear much talk about angels or devils. In my growing up experience if we ever talked about angels it was to praise a person who had helped us — "He was such an angel for fixing our car." If we talked about demons it was in the context of moods, depression and anxiety. I never heard about angels for who they really were, and if the preacher mentioned them it was always in the past tense. They were forever encased in the stained glass, with halos over their heads and wings on their backs — a pretty picture, but not very useful.

When the Church began to realize, especially through missionary testimonies, that there was another world made up of demons and angels, they swung the other way and began to focus on demons. A number of books about demons appeared, and people seemed to forget that only one-third of the angels fell from Heaven and became demons, or fallen angels. Two-thirds of the angels remained faithful.

Some Christians began to pay attention to demons while ignoring the plan and purpose God has given to faithful angels. A morbid fascination with demons took over in some churches, causing people to be afraid of supernatural things or to shrink back from the subject of angels altogether. And yet the book of Acts records more experiences with angels than with demons.

Today when you talk about angels, some will still say you are insane. Jesus and most of His followers were called crazy for the supernatural experiences they had. And yet today, because of the popularity of angels, there are many open doors for Christians to speak about God and angels in a way that brings truth to people who do not know Christ.

So, what are angels? How do we characterize them? In the next chapter we will begin to answer that question.

Chapter 2

Good Angels

Angels are involved every day, every moment, in the affairs of men. There is a constant stream of angels coming to earth and leaving the earth. Some day when we are in Heaven and our eyes are fully opened to what really took place on earth, we will be astonished at how much angelic involvement there was, most of which we did not recognize.

Unfortunately, most people do not know what the Bible says about angels, so they believe popular opinion or ungodly teachings. Contrary to popular sentiment, angels are not bare-bottom cupids, or infants with wings as some paintings depict. They are not effeminate creatures. In fact, no matter what the greeting card companies say, the Bible never depicts angels as women. They are always depicted in the masculine, even though the Bible tells us that angels do not marry and apparently do not have romantic relationships.

Angels are not fairies, disembodied spirits, elves, sprites, ghosts, leprechauns, birds, mythical creatures, or half-humans. They are not ethereal beings existing in a godless netherworld.

God created angels to reflect His glory, carry out His will on earth and Heaven, worship Him, bring messages, and partner with God and men to accomplish His purposes in the earth. Unlike the benign, wimpy, self-motivated angels popular in our culture, real angels are:

- powerful

- obedient

- awe-inspiring

- incredibly majestic

After all, angels live in Heaven which is permeated by God's presence, power and might, and they carry that presence, power, and might with them when they visit the earth.

What Angels Look Like

The word "angel" in Hebrew is the word for "messenger." Angels are simply messengers. They come from Heaven. They travel at the speed of thought.

As quickly as you can think "California" or "Florida" they can arrive there. They are deputies, dispatched ones, ambassadors bringing messages from God. The writer of Hebrews says:

> ...He makes his angels winds, his servants flames of fire.
>
> —Hebrews 1:7

What do angels look like? The Old Testament gives us a glimpse of them. In Isaiah six, the prophet describes the angels in the throne room of God.

> In the year that King Uzziah died, I saw the LORD seated on a throne, high and exalted, and the train of his robe filled the temple. Above him were seraphs, each with six wings: With two wings they covered their faces, with two they covered their feet, and with two they were flying. And they were calling to one another: "Holy, holy, holy is the LORD Almighty; the whole earth is full of his glory."
>
> At the sound of their voices the doorposts and thresholds shook and the temple was filled with smoke.
>
> "Woe to me!" I cried. "I am ruined! For I am a man of unclean lips, and I live among a people of unclean lips, and my eyes have seen the King, the LORD Almighty."
>
> Then one of the seraphs flew to me with a live coal in his hand, which he had taken with tongs from the altar. With it he touched my mouth and said, "See, this has touched your lips; your guilt is taken away and your sin atoned for."
>
> —Isaiah 6:1-7

Interesting Facts About Angels

Not only do angels look different than us, they have their own language, as Paul noted in the famous "love" passage from 1 Corinthians.

> If I speak in the tongues of men *and of angels*, but have not love, I am only a resounding gong or a clanging cymbal.
>
> —1 Corinthians 13:1 (italics added)

Angels assisted God in giving the law of the Old Testament to the Hebrews. Paul said in Galatians 3:19 that the law was put into effect through angels by a mediator.

Angels do not die.

> But those who are considered worthy of taking part in that age and in the resurrection from the dead will neither marry nor be given in marriage, and *they can no longer die; for they are like the angels.* They are God's children, since they are children of the resurrection.
>
> —Luke 20:35-36 (italics added)

The Bible seems to indicate that there are different types of angels for different tasks. Some are warrior angels and are pictured with swords, as when God put an angel at the entrance to the Garden of Eden.

> After he drove the man out, he placed on the east side of the Garden of Eden cherubim and a flaming sword flashing back and forth to guard the way to the tree of life.
>
> —Genesis 3:24

And elsewhere:

> Then the LORD opened the eyes of Balaam, and he saw the angel of the LORD standing in the way, and his sword drawn in his hand: and he bowed down his head, and fell flat on his face.

> —Numbers 22:31 (KJV)

But angels are not all-powerful. God is clearly the One directing their activities, and it is for His Name's sake and His glory that they exist. The writer of Hebrews spoke of Jesus when he wrote:

> So he became as much superior to the angels as the name he has inherited is superior to theirs. For to which of the angels did God ever say, "You are my Son; today I have become your Father"? Or again, "I will be his Father, and he will be my Son"? And again, when God brings his firstborn into the world, he says, "Let all God's angels worship him."

> —Hebrews 1:4-6

Angels And Humans

Humans actually have a higher place in God's hierarchy of created beings. We were made a little lower than the angels, but when we accept Christ, we are recreated and ascend to a place a little higher than the angels.

> It is not to angels that he has subjected the world to come, about which we are speaking.

> —Hebrews 2:5

> Do you not know that we will judge angels? How
> much more the things of this life!
>
> —1 Corinthians 6:3

Humans and angels are entirely different creatures. An angel can never become human, nor can a
human become an angel. Angels are not highly
evolved humans. Demons are not bad people who
have died and come back to haunt us. There is no
crossover.

Angels are very curious about humans, this other
creature God made. They love to look intently into
things concerning salvation and what makes us tick.

> Concerning this salvation, the prophets, who
> spoke of the grace that was to come to you,
> searched intently and with the greatest care, try-
> ing to find out the time and circumstances to
> which the Spirit of Christ in them was pointing
> when he predicted the sufferings of Christ and
> the glories that would follow. It was revealed to
> them that they were not serving themselves but
> you, when they spoke of the things that have
> now been told you by those who have preached
> the gospel to you by the Holy Spirit sent from
> heaven. *Even angels long to look into these things.*
>
> —1 Peter 1:10-12 (italics added)

It might be true that angels are just as curious
about us as we are about them!

Angels And God's Glory

Angels seem to play a large role in declaring and
witnessing God's glory. They gather about the throne

and worship for all eternity saying, "Holy, holy, holy!" (Revelation 4:8) Angels also are witnesses of God's interactions with men. Jesus said:

> For the Son of Man is going to come in his Father's glory with his angels, and then he will reward each person according to what he has done.
>
> —Matthew 16:27

> See that you do not look down on one of these little ones. For I tell you that their angels in heaven always see the face of my Father in heaven.
>
> —Matthew 18:10

> If anyone is ashamed of me and my words in this adulterous and sinful generation, the Son of Man will be ashamed of him when he comes in his Father's glory with the holy angels.
>
> —Mark 8:38

> I tell you, whoever acknowledges me before men, the Son of Man will also acknowledge him before the angels of God. But he who disowns me before men will be disowned before the angels of God.
>
> —Luke 12:8-9

Jesus placed great importance on whether we would be acknowledged or disowned before the angels of God. Why? We probably won't know until we get there, but I imagine that it is because angels are faithful witnesses to how God deals with men. Because they live in the presence of God they can testify to His perfect judgments.

In the coming chapters we will look more extensively at what angels do on earth, but first we turn our attention to another group of angels that figure largely into human affairs: disobedient angels, or what the Bible calls *demons*.

Chapter 3

Bad Angels

... God did not spare angels when they sinned, but sent them to hell, putting them into gloomy dungeons to be held for judgment;

—2 Peter 2:4

And no wonder, for Satan himself masquerades as an angel of light.

—2 Corinthians 11:14

One of the most dangerous beliefs about angels is that they are all good, when in fact a third of the created angels are quite evil. Not all visitors from the supernatural realm can be trusted. It runs against the current mindset to realize that a third of the angels God created are actually working against us, trying to keep us out of Heaven, but that is exactly the case.

The word "angel" can refer to God's obedient angels or to angels who disobeyed God, which are called demons. In the rest of this book we will refer to God's angels — the faithful ones — simply as angels, and the devil's angels as demons. But be wary of those who use the word "angel" loosely and without defining it. They may be including demons in their "spirituality" without knowing it.

The Angels Who Fell

The Bible gives us a fascinating account of how the angels came to be divided into good and bad.

> A great and wondrous sign appeared in heaven: a woman clothed with the sun, with the moon under her feet and a crown of twelve stars on her head. She was pregnant and cried out in pain as she was about to give birth.
>
> Then another sign appeared in heaven: an enormous red dragon with seven heads and ten horns and seven crowns on his heads. His tail swept a third of the stars out of the sky and flung them to the earth. The dragon stood in front of the woman who was about to give birth, so that he might devour her child the moment it was born.
>
> She gave birth to a son, a male child, who will rule all the nations with an iron scepter. And her child was snatched up to God and to his throne. The woman fled into the desert to a place prepared for her by God, where she might be taken care of for 1,260 days.
>
> And there was war in heaven. Michael and his angels fought against the dragon, and the dragon and his angels fought back. But he was not strong enough, and they lost their place in

heaven. The great dragon was hurled down—that ancient serpent called the devil, or Satan, who leads the whole world astray. He was hurled to the earth, and his angels with him.

Then I heard a loud voice in heaven say: "Now have come the salvation and the power and the kingdom of our God, and the authority of his Christ. For the accuser of our brothers, who accuses them before our God day and night, has been hurled down. They overcame him by the blood of the Lamb and by the word of their testimony; they did not love their lives so much as to shrink from death. Therefore rejoice, you heavens and you who dwell in them! But woe to the earth and the sea, because the devil has gone down to you! He is filled with fury, because he knows that his time is short."

When the dragon saw that he had been hurled to the earth, he pursued the woman who had given birth to the male child. The woman was given the two wings of a great eagle, so that she might fly to the place prepared for her in the desert, where she would be taken care of for a time, times and half a time, out of the serpent's reach.

Then from his mouth the serpent spewed water like a river, to overtake the woman and sweep her away with the torrent. But the earth helped the woman by opening its mouth and swallowing the river that the dragon had spewed out of his mouth. Then the dragon was enraged at the woman and went off to make war against the rest of her offspring—those who obey God's commandments and hold to the testimony of Jesus.

—Revelation 12:1-17

Here we have a clear picture of two invisible armies. We have Michael leading the warrior angels of almighty God; and we have the dragon also known as the accuser, Satan, the leader of dark, fallen angels. These two angelic forces are at war even as we speak.

What do demons do? Try to kill people! They cannot possibly defeat God, so they go after His cherished creation. Their one single goal is to get as many people into hell as possible. Hell was created especially for demons, not for people, even though people who do not accept Christ will end up there. One day Satan and all the angels who followed him will be cast into hell, but until then they try to deceive, blind, and lead people astray.

We see this throughout the Gospels. Demons made people sick, suicidal, insane, mute, blind, even hunched over. The list of what demons do to harm people goes on and on, but suffice it to say that God is much greater than demons and has dispatched His holy angels to protect, lead, and defend us against them. Luke, chapters one and two, tells of the times that angels warned Mary and Joseph of demonic plots against them. The book of Acts also shows us how angels thwart the plans of the enemy and help the spread of the Gospel.

Angels Of Light

It is not uncommon to hear people testify about an experience they had with an angel. It is not uncommon to meet people who say they talk to angels. But not all of these experiences are valid or godly. The New Age religion, which is just another name for the occult, makes no distinction between good angels and bad angels and leads many people into dangerous waters.

I began this chapter with a quote from Paul who said that Satan can transform himself into an angel of light to bring deception, tragedy and destruction into human lives. Sadly, many people believe that any being that appears to them from the world beyond, must be benevolent or harmless. This is far from true.

Most of the current books about angels in the secular market are not talking about heavenly angels; they are talking about what the Old Testament called "familiar spirits." Moses told the people of God that if they dealt in familiar spirits they would be cut off from God's people and from the promised land (Leviticus 20:6 KJV).

What are familiar spirits? They are demons, impostor spirits, lying spirits. They claim to be something they are not. Sometimes they claim to be disembodied human spirits. In the Old Testament, mediums and witches would conjure up so-called spirits of the dead. The Bible tells us they were not spirits of the dead but "familiar spirits" or demons who would imitate people who had died.

> Do not turn to mediums or seek out spiritists, for you will be defiled by them. I am the LORD your God.
>
> —Leviticus 19:31

> I will set my face against the person who turns to mediums and spiritists to prostitute himself by following them, and I will cut him off from his people.
>
> —Leviticus 20:6

> Let no one be found among you who sacrifices his son or daughter in the fire, who practices divination or sorcery, interprets omens, engages in witchcraft, or casts spells, or who is a medium or spiritist or who consults the dead.
>
> Anyone who does these things is detestable to the LORD, and because of these detestable practices the LORD your God will drive out those nations before you.
>
> —Deuteronomy 18:10-12

Why are we forbidden from dealing with them? Because God intended only one Man to be the mediator between God and men, and He is Jesus Christ. To deal with familiar spirits is to give them the honor accorded only to Jesus.

> For there is one God and one mediator between
> God and men, the man Christ Jesus.
>
> —1 Timothy 2:5

Not only that, but God knows that demons intend to harm and kill us.

Communicating with "the dead" — which are really familiar spirits — became popular after World War II when people wanted to contact loved ones who had died in the war.

Then came the New Age movement which popularized the idea of "spirit guides," which is another name for familiar spirits. New Age teachers told followers to conjure up a spirit guide that would lead them through life — a blatantly anti-Christian idea. Oftentimes these "guides" were called "angels," and in a sense they were correct, because the guides were nothing more than demons, posing as other worldly beings. The word "angel" was hijacked and abused, leading to much confusion about what an angel really is.

Telling The Difference

Today there is no shortage of religions or spiritual practices that embrace angels but reject Jesus. These "new" religions are really old religions repackaged and re-sold. They are just as ungodly now as they were then, and they still rely on familiar spirits — demons posing as angels or dead people.

We have to go to God's Word to find out the difference between angels and demons. Jesus said two men built houses, one on the sand, one on the rock. The storms came, and one house was leveled while the other stood firm. What was the difference? One built his house on popular opinion and personal experience — "I think this, I think that. So-and-so told me this. I read a book that said such-and-such. I saw someone say this on Oprah."

The other built his house on the Word of God.

One was susceptible to demonic persuasion; the other knew how to spot an impostor.

How do we differentiate between demons and angels? This is a key question for any Christian, because both good and bad angels interact with us and can affect our lives directly. In the next chapter we will gain clear insight on this question as we discuss the nine things a good angel will never do.

Chapter 4

Nine Things A Good Angel Will Never Do

Rhonda walked into the living room where the other potluck guests were socializing. The buzz of conversation told her again how blessed she was to belong to a church where people were friends and enjoyed getting together for more than Sunday and mid-week services.

She walked to the food table to pour herself some lemonade and then joined three ladies who were having a discussion nearby.

"I see them whenever it rains," said Benicia, an excitable woman Rhonda knew from Sunday school. "Little angels dancing on the leaves of the trees. Oh, they are so adorable! I guess God knew I just needed to see angels on some days to get me through."

The other women sipped their hot tea and listened. Mary piped up.

"My aunt used to say she saw ballerina angels dancing around the foot of her bed," she said. "She said they came to entertain her whenever she felt down."

"I believe that," Benicia said quickly.

"Well, I saw a talk show on television, and the woman there said she had a long friendship with an angel who would visit her for coffee each afternoon and tell her secrets," said Claire, the third woman in the group.

Benicia looked at her skeptically.

"I don't know about that," she said. "You can't believe everything you hear about angels, especially from non-believers. But I sure am glad God shows me those angels on the trees when it rains."

Rhonda went to re-fill her cup and felt slightly dizzy from the conversation she had listened to. Did angels really dance on the leaves when it rained? Did people really have angel acquaintances? And what about ballerina angels? What should she believe? Who was telling the truth?

Strange Ideas

If you have ever been in such a conversation you know how hazy the facts can get. Even well-meaning, sincere Christians can hold strange beliefs about angels. It does not mean they are not saved, but that, like the rest of us, they have parts of their theology or experience that don't yet line up with the truth.

How do we know who is telling the truth? Which ideas are for real and which are ungodly? Getting to the bottom of strange angel ideas is fairly easy: If it does not level with God's Word, it is not true.

But let's sharpen our concept of what a good angel does by looking at nine things a good angel will never do.

■ *Number one: Angels never chit-chat.*

Have you ever wanted God to lift the veil off the spirit world and show you the angels all around you? Have you wanted to have a long conversation with an angel about what Heaven is like? Has your curiosity ever prompted you to wish you could communicate — just once — with one of these supernatural beings? It is natural to want that, and I believe that in Heaven we will have many conversations with angels.

But for now it is important to understand that angels never chit-chat with human beings. Angels never speak of their own volition. They are not self-employed, they do not have the luxury of dropping by for tea or watching the ball game with you and shooting the breeze. Angels simply are not chatty.

People who say they chat with angels are probably chatting with demons. Demons are always talking about trivia and things that mean nothing because demons no longer have standing or purpose with God. Demons are unemployed and have all the time in the world to waste.

Angels have other missions, other tasks to take care of, and they are strictly forbidden from acting or speaking anything other than what God wants them to do or say. Nowhere in the Bible do you find angels dropping by to talk without some purpose in mind.

And, just to clear this up, nowhere in the Bible do we find the idea of an angel on your shoulder, telling you what to do. God has given us consciences and the Holy Spirit to bring conviction. He does not need to put an angel on your shoulder.

Angels say what they have to say and then they leave. Any other kind of angel is a demon trying to deceive.

■   *Number two: Angels never accept praise or worship.*

> Do not let anyone who delights in false humil-
> ity and the worship of angels disqualify you for
> the prize. Such a person goes into great detail
> about what he has seen, and his unspiritual
> mind puffs him up with idle notions.
>
> —Colossians 2:18

An angel will never accept praise or worship from anyone — not a fellow angel, not a human being. This was at the heart of Satan's corruption. Satan was an angel at one time and he could not stand everybody worshiping God. In his heart was pride, and out of that pride grew rebellion, and because of that rebellion he paid an eternal price and became the miserable creature that he is today.

In Revelation 22:8-9, when John was in the midst of a mighty vision of the future, he was compelled to fall down and worship the angel that was with him. It is not difficult to see why. Angels live in the presence of God, and some of that glory rubs off on them.

The same is true of you and me. When we are in God's presence, it rubs off on us and we glow with His glory the same way Moses did when he came down from the mountain of God.

But when John fell at the angel's feet, (and he did it more than once,) the angel said:

> "Do not do it! I am a fellow servant with you
> and with your brothers the prophets and of all
> who keep the words of this book. Worship God!"

God said:

> Do not worship any other god, for the LORD,
> whose name is Jealous, is a jealous God.
>
> —**Exodus 34:14**

In Judges 13:15-16b we find the story of an angel appearing to the parents of Samson, (before Samson was born,) and telling them that Samson was never to drink wine or cut his hair.

> Manoah said to the angel of the LORD, "We
> would like you to stay until we prepare a young
> goat for you." The angel of the LORD replied,
> "Even though you detain me, I will not eat any
> of your food. But if you prepare a burnt offering,
> offer it to the LORD."

The angel would not allow himself to be worshiped, demonstrating that he was a faithful angel of God.

I was talking with a member of my church who got up one morning and felt impressed to pray for his daughter who lived in a mobile home park. He did not know why, and he had never prayed this way before, but he prayed, "Dear God, surround Susan with angels."

Susan happened to leave something burning on her stove that day. She went off to sleep and the stove caught fire. Her mobile home was in flames, and out of nowhere a man walked through the front door, but Susan's dog did not bark at him. He picked up Susan, took her and her dog out of the house as it burned to ashes, and then disappeared. She tried to find him later, but none of the neighbors had seen him.

Susan and her father believe it was an angel that carried her through the fire that day, and I believe them. You see, angels never want to be thanked. They refuse to be worshiped. They do the job God sent them to do, and then they go.

Angels will not change the Scriptures, and will never introduce another gospel!

Chapter 5

Angels And The Real Gospel

■ *The third thing an angel of God will never do is corrupt important relationships.*

One of the hallmarks of demonic involvement is that important relationships are harmed. Think of the demonized people in the New Testament — the man who lived among the tombs and cut himself with rocks certainly had lost his family relationships. Mary Magdalene, from whom seven demons came out, was probably a prostitute and her very business was in corrupt relationships. You never find someone who is involved with demons whose life and relationships are intact.

Many people are discovering today that the "spirit guides" who were supposed to lead them into spiritual knowledge or revelation have destroyed their families. Though it seems cutting edge, demons will always put a wedge in important relationships, somehow, some way, at their earliest opportunity.

How do I know this?

> For our struggle is not against flesh and blood, but against the rulers, against the authorities, against the powers of this dark world and against the spiritual forces of evil in the heavenly realms.
>
> —Ephesians 6:12

That verse is well-known, but the train of thought actually starts in Ephesians, chapter five, and goes through the first few verses of chapter six, and it is talking about important relationships.

> … each one of you also must love his wife as he loves himself, and the wife must respect her husband. Children, obey your parents in the Lord, for this is right. "Honor your father and mother"—which is the first commandment with a promise — "that it may go well with you and that you may enjoy long life on the earth." Fathers, do not exasperate your children; instead, bring them up in the training and instruction of the Lord.
>
> —Ephesians 5:33-6:4

Paul covers most important relationships in this passage before going into, "our struggle is not against flesh and blood." Why? Because a main tactic of the enemy is to corrupt relationships. Maintaining healthy relationships with our spouse, children, employer, and pastor is a big part of spiritual warfare. If you are fighting with your husband or wife, don't think you can lock yourself away in the bedroom and do battle on behalf of God's Kingdom. No, the enemy is in your very camp!

There is a picture of this in Revelation 12 when the woman in John's vision is about to give birth to a man-child. She has travailed and the baby is about to be born, and standing there ready to gobble the baby up is the dragon, the devil.

To me this signifies the devil's intention to disrupt and corrupt relationships right before God does something important. I have found that when God is about to move in a powerful way, Christian relationships start coming under attack. When people are coming to Christ and revival is flowing at my church, that is when I am more tense and edgy, and I am quicker to snap at my wife. It happens with husbands and wives, children and parents, employers and employees. Part of it is natural — we get tired — but part of it is the devil who whispers things to us, and if we do not cast them down as from a demon, then we begin to dwell on them. And when we begin to dwell on them, they take root. When they take root, relationships are corrupted.

Good angels never corrupt important relationships. They are there to support, encourage, uplift and sow seeds of unity among brethren. Never will an angel visit you and say something to cut you off from the important relationships in your life.

■   *Number four: Angels never introduce another gospel or changes to the Scriptures.*

Have you ever wondered why there are so many ungodly religions and cults in the world? Why do people believe them with such fervor? It is not just because people have a spirit and yearn for something spiritual, but that these religions and cults actually originated in the spirit world and were founded by demons. The beliefs, though wrong, have a spiritual power that undiscerning people cannot distinguish from the true Gospel.

It is possible for demons to introduce whole religious systems. Entire cults have been founded by people who opened themselves up to demonic influence and received strange doctrines from fallen angels.

> The Spirit clearly says that in later times some will abandon the faith and follow deceiving spirits and things taught by demons.
>
> —1 Timothy 4:1

One American cult was founded by a man who said an angel gave him ten golden tablets upon which were written so-called new truths from God. That cult is thriving all over the world and advertises on television saying there is another gospel and a new book that is divinely inspired. Millions have gone astray because a demon was able to convince one man to add to the Gospel of Christ. This particular cult says, and I quote: "Angels have always been a source of revelation for new truth."

That is utterly false. Angels have never been a source for new truth. They have revealed God's truth at key moments in biblical times, but they have never been a source for truth, and now that Scripture has been written and God has sealed it — meaning it cannot be added to or subtracted from — nothing new will ever be added. Good angels will never change the Scriptures and never introduce another gospel.

Indeed, there is no new truth.

> ...I am the way and the truth and the life. No one comes to the Father except through me.
>
> —John 14:6

Ecclesiastes says there is nothing new under the sun (1:9). If angels try to introduce a new truth — even if they talk in King James English — they are not angels but demons.

Paul wrote about this in his letter to the Galatian church. The Galatians were experiencing the glorious grace of God. They realized that no religion in the world could save them — no works, no deeds, no promises made. They realized that all their efforts were like filthy rags because what Jesus did on the cross was good enough.

Then along came the Judaizers, spiritual abusers who said, "Yes, you are saved by grace, but you are kept saved by your works and what you do. Your standing with God is only as secure as your daily walk."

It was a strong argument because every one of us knows that we don't deserve God's grace, and it seems logical that we ought to earn it with daily good works. But if our salvation depends on our daily walk, every one of us is sunk. The Judaizers said that Paul was not really spiritual because he was trusting in grace, and they actually called him a licentious preacher, accusing him of giving people permission to do anything they wanted. In response, Paul wrote these words:

> I am astonished that you are so quickly deserting the one who called you by the grace of Christ and are turning to a different gospel — which is really no gospel at all. Evidently some people are throwing you into confusion and are trying to pervert the gospel of Christ. But even if we *or*

an angel from heaven should preach a gospel
other than the one we preached to you, let him
be eternally condemned!

—Galatians 1:6-8 (italics added)

Paul was not just using strong language to make a point; he knew that demons are ready and willing to introduce new "gospels."

A Deceived Pastor

A young pastor became sick and was laying in bed when the room was filled with a brilliant light, and at the end of his bed was this glowing creature. The creature said, "I have been sent by God to tell you that you are going to die of this sickness, and when you do, great glory will be brought to the Heavenly Father."

The pastor said, "That is wonderful." He was relieved and excited to be going to Heaven. He started telling everybody about his experience. "It was so glorious," he said. "This angel from God appeared at the end of my bed and told me my sickness was going to kill me and God was going to get glory out of it."

Finally, a couple of ministers said, "Pastor, did what that angel say to you line up with the Word of God?"

The man protested, "It had to be an angel from God because he was so brilliant and radiant, and I felt so much warmth when he came in the room."

They said, "Nowhere in God's Word does it say that God gets glory out of sickness and death. Glory was always brought to God when people were healed and made well. Read the Gospels. Even the man that was born blind, Jesus said, was so the glory of God would be manifest not in his sickness but in his healing."

All of a sudden it dawned on him, and the pastor said, "I believed a lie. I believed an experience more than I believed God's Word." He renounced the experience, the ministers prayed for him and a heat came from the top of his head down to the soles of his feet and he was healed. He is still preaching the Gospel today!

What if he had believed the lies of that creature disguised as an angel? He would probably be dead today.

Angels will not change the Scriptures, and will never introduce another gospel!

Chapter 6

Praying To Angels?

■ *The fifth thing an angel will never do is receive or answer requests.*

Good angels never respond to a person's prayer to them. Nowhere in the Bible do we find a person who calls out to angels for help, as some people do today. Whenever a person calls out to angels for help, demons respond because we are to worship and pray to God alone.

I heard a lady talking one day, and I said, "Who are you talking to?" She said, "I am talking to my angel. His name is Michael." I thought sarcastically, "She must really be important to have Michael the archangel, the head of all the warrior angels, as her personal assistant."

New Age religions teach that you can talk to angels, get them to come into your life, and accept them into your body. Those are not angels, they are demons! But nobody would go to a seminar on "How To Become Demon Possessed." Rather they have seminars on "How To Become Angel Possessed," and they give steps to contacting your angel. I could quote their brochure here, but I don't want to give their false theology any more publicity.

Good angels never respond to our call to them. They will respond, however, when we call to God because they respond only to God's orders. God monitors the earth, and when there is a problem He dispatches angels; we cannot dispatch the angels. I cannot find any place in Scripture where human beings sent angels to do anything.

Angel Worship

I received a letter in the mail one time that said, "Be healthier and happier. Invoke your guardian angels." It talked about a woman doctor who said she witnessed medical miracles when people harnessed the power of angels to cure themselves. The letter went on to say, "Dear friend, a scientist who talks with angels? Every day, Dr. Pamela invokes the angel Michael on her left side and asks him to help her be lovable and loving."

The Bible says the Holy Spirit sheds abroad God's love in our hearts, not the angel Michael (Romans 5:5).

The letter continued, "She calls the angel Gabriel to her right side to help her overcome fear, anxiety and stress. In front of her is Urial, the angel of a clear mind." Yet the Bible says:

> **For God hath not given us the spirit of fear; but of power, and of love, and of a sound mind.**
>
> **—2 Timothy 1:7 (KJV)**

"If she has an ache, a pain or a worry, she invites Raphael into the specific area of her mind or body that needs to come into wholeness."

The letter was promoting angel worship, exactly what Satan wants! Angels are never objects of worship or objects of prayer. They deliver answers to prayer but are never the objects.

Demonized Adolf Hitler

I was watching a documentary on Hitler and was amazed at how women screamed and cried when they saw him. He held people in a kind of spell and demanded absolute worship from them. They did not know, I am sure, that it was worship, but they had to raise their hand and hail him.

As Hitler started making progress in Europe, a missionary in France named Kenneth, and his wife Suzanne, were hiding Jews and getting them into Switzerland. Kenneth found out that he was on the wanted list by the Nazis and he narrowly escaped with his wife into Switzerland.

They did not have much money. They lived in an apartment complex. One night there was nothing to cook for dinner, so Suzanne sat down and made a dream list of what she would cook if she had it: five pounds of Gold Medal flour, two pounds of sugar, cheddar cheese, bread … She got on her knees and said, "Dear Jesus, would you send me these things?"

A knock came at the door and there was a tall man wearing a blue shopkeeper's apron and he said, "I am here to deliver the groceries you ordered." She said, "There must be some mistake. I did not order any groceries."

Fear gripped her because she did not have money to pay him, but he said, "No, you ordered these groceries, and they are already paid for." He walked right into the house, put them down on the kitchen table and started pulling things out: five pounds of Gold Medal flour, two pounds of sugar, cheddar cheese … everything she prayed for. The man walked out and Kenneth ran over to the window of the hallway. There was no other way to leave the apartment, but the man never went by that window. He had vanished.

The point is this: She did not pray to the angel, she prayed to Jesus, and Jesus ordered the angel to make the delivery!

We do not pray to angels because the Bible says there is only one mediator between God and man and that is Christ Jesus. When we focus on Jesus and give Him preeminence and make Him Lord of our lives, we get the help of angels, too.

■ *Number six: Angels never try to convince you of their might, intelligence, or omnipresence.*

Angels are powerful but they are not almighty. They exude strength and dignity, but their strength is limited. They are intelligent but not all-knowing. They are fast but not omnipresent. Only God is omnipresent, and can be every place at one time. Only God is omniscient, and knows everything. Only God is all-powerful.

If you study angels in the Bible, you find that they are humble, submissive, and do not require thanks — and they never try to convince you of the superiority of their own attributes. They only want to serve God and get the job done. They recognize the limits of their strength, intelligence and abilities.

In the book of Acts we find a good example of this:

> It was about this time that King Herod arrested some who belonged to the church, intending to persecute them. He had James, the brother of John, put to death with the sword. When he saw that this pleased the Jews, he proceeded to seize Peter also. This happened during the Feast of Unleavened Bread.
>
> After arresting him, he put him in prison, handing him over to be guarded by four squads of four soldiers each. Herod intended to bring him out for public trial after the Passover. So Peter was kept in prison, but the church was earnestly praying to God for him.
>
> The night before Herod was to bring him to trial, Peter was sleeping between two soldiers, bound with two chains, and sentries stood guard at the entrance. Suddenly an angel of the Lord appeared and a light shone in the cell. He struck Peter on the side and woke him up. "Quick, get up!" he said, and the chains fell off Peter's wrists. Then the angel said to him, "Put on your clothes and sandals." And Peter did so. "Wrap your cloak around you and follow me," the angel told him.
>
> Peter followed him out of the prison, but he had no idea that what the angel was doing was really happening; he thought he was seeing a vision.
>
> They passed the first and second guards and came to the iron gate leading to the city. It opened for them by itself, and they went through it. When they had walked the length of one street, suddenly the angel left him.

Then Peter came to himself and said, "Now I
know without a doubt that the Lord sent his angel and rescued me from Herod's clutches and
from everything the Jewish people were antici-
pating."

—Acts 12:1-11

The angel did not try to impress Peter with his
ability to break the shackles or open the gates without a word. You see, angels aren't interested in taking any credit or any glory. They are so unlike humans. We usually want to hang around, receive a
reward, have dinner, convince everyone of our
strength and intelligence. But angels are not interested in angel biographies. They do not want any
glory and will not try to enhance their reputations in
our eyes. If an angel tries to impress, we can be sure
he is from the enemy's side.

Any angel that tries to make someone feel that he has no choice about an issue is a deceiving angel, a demon.

Chapter 7

Angels And UFOs

The seventh thing an angel will never do is violate the free will of humans.

Free will is a sacred right God has given to men and women. Even God Himself will not take that right away. Angels can warn, stand in your way, do everything to stop you, but if you choose to go ahead, there is nothing they can do because God made us to be free moral agents. We are not computers or programmable dolls.

Any angel that tries to make someone feel that he has no choice about an issue is a deceiving angel, a demon.

◼ *Number eight: Angels never act in ways beyond what the Bible reveals about them.*

Some people say angels give them the strength to bend spoons with their mind or perform other supernatural feats. Those are demons. God's angels never stray from their God-ordained roles. In the Bible we see that they have clearly defined purposes as servants and worshipers of God. Everything they do flows from those two purposes. We will talk more about those roles later.

◼ *Number nine: Angels never stir up fascination with the paranormal.*

UFOs, ghosts, science fiction, a compulsive fascination with exorcism — none of these come from Heaven or angels. You see, angels are always pointing to Jesus Christ, not to weird or mysterious occurrences.

I believe that if there are UFOs, they are explicable in natural terms, or they are demonic. Why would demons manifest as UFOs? To deceive the world, to lead people into fascination with the paranormal. When that happens, there is trouble around the corner.

In the 1950s a famous Episcopal bishop became interested in the paranormal and in demons. He began attending seances and reading about spiritism. His son had died and the bishop wanted to talk to him, and at one of the seances a demon imitating the voice of his son began speaking. Before it was all said and done, the bishop was denying the deity of Jesus Christ. He went to Israel to find hidden scrolls to prove that Jesus was not divine, and while he was in the desert, his car broke down and he died.

When you fool with angels from the dark side, they will lead you on for a while, and then the snare will be drawn in and you will lose your life.

Good angels never try to stir up a fascination in the paranormal.

In studies done of victims of rape and violent crime, a large percentage of them had a morbid interest in horror movies. Could it be that this presence or spiritual residue from horror and paranormal movies attracts the attention of a criminal, marking someone as easy prey? We can't say that for sure, and it isn't always true, but I do believe that immersing oneself in paranormal topics or practices leads right into the hands of the devil.

Let's recap the nine things an angel will never do:

■ *Number one:* Angels never chit-chat.

■　　*Number two:* Angels never accept praise or worship.

■　　*Number three:* Angels never corrupt important relationships.

■　　*Number four:* Angels never introduce another gospel or changes to the Scriptures.

■　　*Number five:* Angels never receive or answer requests.

■　　*Number six:* Angels never try to convince you of their might, intelligence or omnipresence.

■　　*Number seven:* Angels never violate the free will of humans.

■　　*Number eight:* Angels never act in ways beyond what the Bible reveals about them.

■　　*Number nine:* Angels never stir up fascination with the paranormal.

Now, let's look at thirteen things angels always do.

Chapter 8

Thirteen Things Angels Always Do

Angels are busy creatures. The Bible never gives us a picture of angels waiting around the water cooler. They are always acting, singing, praising, delivering messages, intervening, chasing, surrounding, protecting.

What exactly do angels do? The Bible is full of answers. In the ministry of Jesus, angels:

- announced His birth.

- provided protection for Mary and Joseph, and warned them to go to Egypt to escape Herod.

- brought comfort to Jesus after He was tempted.

- ministered to Him in the garden of Gethsemane.

- appeared with Him in the transfiguration.

- announced His resurrection.

- instructed the disciples right after He ascended into Heaven.

In addition, we know they work behind the scenes in the drama of world events to convey blessings or to execute judgment. But let's discuss these one at a time so we get a clear understanding of what angels do, and how they are involved in our lives.

■ *Number one: Angels come to dinner.*

This may surprise you, but the Bible says:

> **Do not forget to entertain strangers, for by so doing some people have entertained angels without knowing it.**
>
> **—Hebrews 13:2**

There is a joke about a woman who heard a knock on her door and answered it to find a man she had never seen before. He said, "I need a place to stay for the night."

"You have got to be kidding me," she said.

"No, I do not have any place to sleep, and I thought I would stop here and see if I could stay at your home," he said.

"I am sorry," she said. "You will have to go to the rescue mission."

The man began to fume.

"Don't you know that the Bible says you must entertain strangers because you may be entertaining an angel?" he said.

"I am familiar with that Scripture," the woman replied, "but I am sure that angels do *not* smell like liquor."

Not all angels who say they are angels are really angels. But the Bible does say that angels will mingle among us and even be guests in our homes.

Think of your own life and the people around you. Is it possible that you have come into contact with angels? Some people I meet seem like angels; others seem like devils!

Imagine inviting someone lonely over for dinner — a foreign exchange student, a widow — and one day you get to Heaven and there is an angel that looks a lot like that person. You say, "Aren't you the person we had to dinner?" and he says, "Yes. I was on that assignment on earth. I am an angel and you welcomed me into your home, and now I want to welcome you into my home here in Heaven."

Someday we are going to live among angels, so having them as guests will not be unusual. For now, we do not know who is an angel and who is a human. Our next door neighbor might be an angel. The waitress in the restaurant may be an angel on an assignment.

Before the Bible was even written, Abraham knew to be hospitable. When three angelic beings came to him in the form of humans to let him know about what God had in store for Sodom and Gomorrah, Abraham insisted that they stay for dinner. He foresaw the wisdom in the Scripture quoted above, and he entertained angels for dinner.

I teasingly told my wife one time, "You'd better be good to me because I might not be me. I might be an angel you are entertaining unaware." Maybe that advice will work for you, too!

■   *Number two: Angels Protect Us.*

> **Behold, I send an angel before thee, to keep thee in the way, and to bring thee into the place which I have prepared.**
>
> **—Exodus 23:20 (KJV)**

A boy named Brian and his friends went swimming in a friend's swimming pool on a hot summer day. Then Brian went to work mowing lawns and when he finished his work he thought, "It will feel good to dive in that pool again." He went over to his friend's house but all the lights were out, so he thought, "I'll take a quick dip and then go home." There was no moon that night; it was pitch black. He got onto the diving board and was ready to dive, and a light appeared in the pool. There was an angel with his wings going from one side of the pool to the other.

Brian got off the diving board and knelt at the side the pool to look a little closer, and noticed that the pool had been drained. An angel had appeared and saved his life.

Things like that happen all the time.

> The angel of the LORD encamps around those who fear him, and he delivers them.
>
> —Psalm 34:7

Even Satan acknowledged this when he was tempting Jesus.

> For it is written: 'He will command his angels concerning you to guard you carefully.'
>
> —Luke 4:10

God sends angels to protect those who have accepted Christ or will one day accept Christ. Those who will not come to Christ one day have no such guarantee of protection for them or their families.

The most foolish thing a parent can say is, "I do not bring my children up in any religion. I am going to wait until they are eighteen and let them choose their own beliefs."

That leaves a child unprotected. The best thing a parent can do for a child is raise him or her in the admonition and knowledge of the Lord. I want my kids to have the angels of the Lord camped around about them. I want my property, my family to be guarded by the angels of the Lord.

Amy Semple McPherson was holding a tent crusade and heard that some of the troublemakers in town were going to burn the tent down. She and a group of prayer warriors prayed that God would surround the tent with angels. When the troublemakers came to burn the tent down, they stopped in their tracks and ran off scared. One of them later got saved and said, "We came to burn the tent down until we saw all those angels surrounding it, wing to wing."

The Real Thing

It is a wonderful thing to know you are protected by angels. I had an eye-opening experience one Christmas when I went into a card store and found that at least a third of the cards had angels on them. Not only that, there were angel displays, figurines and pins. The store was selling one crystal angel for three hundred dollars, claiming that it would protect your home. I was glad that I have real angels watching over me, not a few ounces of glass!

Somebody sent me an ad from a catalog about an angel pin that will supposedly protect you if you wear it on your lapel. The pin is in the shape of a little infant with a bare bottom sticking up, and he is carrying a bow and arrow. I am glad I do not have a three-month-old with an arrow as my guardian angel. I would be in real trouble!

Angels are real and they actually protect people in practical ways. You do not need a charm or figurine to give you angelic protection; you simply need to be a follower of Christ. He will surround you with angels — the big, powerful, sturdy kind.

> And when we cried unto the LORD, he heard our voice, and sent an angel, and hath brought us forth out of Egypt: and, behold, we *are* in Kadesh, a city in the uttermost of thy border:
>
> —Numbers 20:16 (KJV)

A mother was washing her dishes one day while her two-and-a-half-year-old daughter played in the living room, and then it dawned on her that she had not heard the girl in a while. She looked out the window, and, to her horror, saw her daughter on the railroad track behind their house, and it was time for the train to come through.

The mother could hear the train whistle blow and feel the vibration. She screamed to Jesus and as she did she saw a tall man dressed in white whisk her daughter to the side of the track. The train went by and the mother ran to get her, but by the time the mother reached her, the man was gone.

An angel had intervened to save that little girl's life.

Seven-year-old Emily walking home from school with her little brother strolled by a big, brick house with an iron fence around it. Intrigued by the house, they stood at the fence when suddenly somebody picked them up and set them several yards away. Just then a speeding car came careening out of control and slammed into the iron fence right where Emily and her little brother had been. They looked around but could not find the man that had picked them up and moved them several yards away.

Some may scoff at such stories, but they happen. Even Daniel, the Old Testament prophet, said it was an angel that held the lion's mouth closed when he was thrown into the lion's den (Daniel 6:21-23).

Saved On The Road To Las Vegas

A young Christian motorcyclist wanted to see Las Vegas, the modern day Sodom and Gomorrah, at night. That probably wasn't a good idea for a few reasons, but he hopped on his motorcycle and began to drive, figuring it would be three o'clock in the morning before he arrived. He was tired as could be, and at 2:30 in the morning he fell asleep on his motorcycle. He was awakened when his front tire hit the jagged rocks on the shoulder and he found himself heading up an embankment at sixty-five miles per hour.

He knew it was all over and he said, "Jesus." Just then, two arms, robed in white, reached out and said, "Let go of the handlebars. I will take it from here." The arms grabbed the handlebars, guided the motorcycle back onto the highway, and when it was safely in control, the arms disappeared. About that time, the man was no longer interested in seeing Las Vegas at night.

An angel had spared his life.

Stuck In The Snow

There is a young pastor who leads a church in Michigan near where I live. He was driving from Charlotte to Lansing on one of those terribly bitter cold days. His wife was home; his kids were with him in the car. The roads were slippery and his car went off the road. The snow was deep, and the car traveled over an embankment and down into a little gully. Nobody could see him from the road, and he was stuck. Anyone who lives in a cold weather climate knows that it is not uncommon to read about someone who went out on a cold night and died because his car broke down.

This pastor knew there was no way they would survive, and he cried, "Jesus, I do not want us to die here. I want my kids to have a life." Just then somebody knocked on his window and said, "Put your hands on the wheel and steer. I am going to push you." The pastor put his hands on the steering wheel, and he felt no bump but the car started moving. The car went forward through deep snow until it went over the big snow bank and onto the road. The pastor got out to thank the man, and nobody was there. He looked behind his car. There were no foot tracks and no tire tracks other than his own.

Angel On The Bus

Patricia was a young teenager. She had a broken heart and decided to leave home. She only had twenty dollars but she got a bus ticket to New York City, and on the way there she developed an incredible toothache. The man sitting in front of her on the bus turned around and said, "Do you have a toothache?" She said, "Yes, it is terrible." He reached into his pocket, pulled something out that she could not see and put it on his finger, then touched her tooth and the pain left. "Do you mind if I sit with you?" he asked, and she said he could.

As they talked she opened up about her life, her brokenness and hurt, and this man comforted her and told her she ought to reconsider her decision to run away.

They got to New York and he said, "Patty, wait right here." He came back and said, "I got you a ticket to go back home. I got me one, too, so I can ride with you." She got on the bus and rode home with that man, then got off the bus and waited for him to get off, but he never did. Today Patty believes he was an angel sent by God to protect her from unknown evils that would have befallen her.

That is the kind of protection we receive from angels who are on assignment from God.

When angels bring messages from God, those messages cause reality to change.

Chapter 9

Messages From Heaven

■ *The third major task angels have is to deliver messages from Heaven.*

Angels delivered many of the prophecies recorded in the Old and New Testaments. In the book of Luke an angel came to Zechariah, father of John the Baptist, and said:

> **Your wife Elizabeth will bear you a son, and you are to give him the name John.**
>
> **—Luke 1:13c**

In a similar way the angel Gabriel came to Mary and told her she would give birth to the Son of God and would call Him Jesus.

An angel appeared to Mary Magdalene and the other Mary when they thought Jesus was in the tomb.

> **After the Sabbath, at dawn on the first day of the week, Mary Magdalene and the other Mary**

went to look at the tomb. There was a violent earthquake, for an angel of the Lord came down from heaven and, going to the tomb, rolled back the stone and sat on it. His appearance was like lightning, and his clothes were white as snow. The guards were so afraid of him that they shook and became like dead men. The angel said to the women, "Do not be afraid, for I know that you are looking for Jesus, who was crucified. He is not here; he has risen, just as he said. Come and see the place where he lay. Then go quickly and tell his disciples: 'He has risen from the dead and is going ahead of you into Galilee. There you will see him.' Now I have told you."

—Matthew 28:1-7

The entire New Testament bursts with incidents of angels delivering messages to believers, telling them what to do, where to go, what to say, who to send on certain mission trips, telling them they would survive certain situations. And I am convinced that they still deliver messages today.

Heavenly Health Insurance

A woman named Phyllis was very sick and didn't have health insurance. She was in Florida taking care of her mother and had not been able to sleep, and this particular night she knew she was going to die. Everything in her cells and body told her the end was near. She finally called the doctor and made an appointment for the next day, but didn't think she could make it. She asked her mother to pray, then went back to bed and said, "Jesus, I do not have any health insurance. The doctor will not see me tonight. If you don't give me a miracle, I know I am not going to make it until the morning."

She lay there and a bright light began to appear at the foot of her bed. Suddenly the silhouette of a man stood there in a glorious, brilliant light, and Phyllis knew he had brought a message from the throne of God. He said to her, "I am not through with you yet." Then he was gone.

Phyllis fell asleep and the next morning went to see the doctor. He ran blood tests and found that she had recently had hepatitis but did not have it any more.

In other words, she had a serious disease the night before, but now it was gone!

When angels bring messages from God, those messages cause reality to change. It is as if the angel is carrying a little box of spiritual plutonium that can obliterate whatever problem or challenge we face.

■   *Number four: Angels assist in bringing loved ones to Christ.*

There are harvesting angels throughout the world assigned to bring people to Christ. Sometimes it involves an individual and sometimes a whole nation.

Even in your family there are harvesting angels working to get your unsaved relatives into Heaven.

Jesus said in explaining the parable of the good soil:

> The field is the world, and the good seed stands for the sons of the kingdom. The weeds are the sons of the evil one, and the enemy who sows them is the devil. The harvest is the end of the age, *and the harvesters are angels.* As the weeds are pulled up and burned in the fire, so it will be at the end of the age. The Son of Man will send out his angels, and they will weed out of his kingdom everything that causes sin and all who do evil. They will throw them into the fiery furnace, where there will be weeping and gnashing of teeth.
>
> —Matthew 13:38-42 (italics added)

Again, He says:

> And he will send his angels and gather his elect from the four winds, from the ends of the earth to the ends of the heavens.
>
> —Mark 13:27

A woman named Karen had no need for God until she was led at gunpoint to a wooded area, raped, shot, and left for dead. It was a few hours before she woke up and realized that she was alive, and she knew she would have to walk all the way to the city to get help. It was an old, gravel, country road.

She gathered her strength but realized there was no way she could make it. She cried out, "God, help me." Just then, somebody picked her up and carried her until they came to a house. Whoever was carrying her knocked on the door. A lady answered the door and, upon seeing Karen, screamed and passed out. Karen must have looked terrible, barefoot and covered with blood.

The man of the house put Karen on the couch and called the paramedics, and when the woman who answered the door came to consciousness, Karen looked at her and said, "I'm sorry I scared you. I must look terrible." The lady said, "It wasn't you that scared me. It was that shining, tall man that was holding you."

When Karen was checked at the hospital, there was not even a scratch on her feet. Somebody carried her. She was not a Christian, but God wanted to save her and He sent an angel to save her life.

Angel In The Jungle

Missionary Ian Trotter tells an amazing story of an African man who lived deep in the jungle and one day thought to himself, "We worship trees and the sun. There must be somebody who made them. I wonder who God is."

Suddenly an angel appeared and said to him, "I am not permitted to preach the Gospel, but if you will go to this village, you will find a building where you hear people singing. There you will learn who God is."

The man ran through the dense forest, came to the village, and there was a church. He walked up to it but the angel stood at the door saying, "Not here." He kept running and found a little run-down building where people were singing. It was the Pentecostal missionary station, and just as he walked in someone began speaking in an unknown tongue. It wasn't unknown to the African man, however, because he was hearing in his own dialect, "All have sinned and come short of the glory of God, and the wages of sin is death. But who so calleth upon the name of the Lord shall be saved. Jesus died on the cross, shedding His blood for your sin. Put your trust in Him. Receive Him as Savior and you will know God, for there is one Mediator between God and man, and that Mediator is the Lord Jesus Christ!"

The man fell down and cried out for Jesus to come into his life, and when he did, he was filled with the Holy Spirit. That is how God can save even those who have never heard the Gospel. He will send a harvesting angel if He has to.

The Man Who Spoke With Angels

In 1982 I was in Charlotte, North Carolina, and met a young man named Ted Buck from Boise, Idaho. Ted's dad was Roland Buck, a man who claimed to have angel visitations. In 1978, when I first heard of Roland Buck, I thought he was a kook. He said angels were coming into his church office to talk to him. They gave him one hundred and twenty prophesies, all of which have come to pass. Even one of the top cult experts in the nation said he could find nothing unscriptural about anything in Buck's experiences.

One day an elderly woman named Bonnie Thompson called Roland Buck and said, "I am calling from San Francisco. I am seventy-nine years old, and you are that guy that has been talking with the angels. I am so distraught. My husband is sick. We have been married for over fifty years, and he drives. I need him. I do not know if he is going to live or die. Maybe you could tell one of those angels to put in a good word for him."

It happened that before she called, Gabriel and a warrior angel had come to Pastor Buck's office, and they were talking to him when the phone rang. The lady did not give her name, but Gabriel said to Pastor Buck, "Tell Bonnie Thompson it is going to be all right." Buck said, "Bonnie Thompson, it is going to be all right," and she started screaming. "Aaahhh! I did not tell you my name! God knows my name! I know everything's going to be all right."

Morris Plotts, a famous missionary in Nairobi, Kenya, was known as Lord Elephant because he had size sixteen shoes. He had an experience where twenty angels came to help him, and when he arrived back in the United States he decided to visit Roland Buck, whom he had not met.

The two hit it off and Plotts related his experience. Buck said, "It is interesting that you would come here because yesterday Gabriel came, and he introduced me to an angel who was stationed in Nairobi, Kenya. This angel said he had not come from Nairobi right then, but from another city on the coast called Massanbuany. The Holy Spirit pulled him out of Nairobi and told him to go there to minister to a family."

Plotts wrote down the dates and times that this angel was there, then went back to Nairobi and decided to see if there really was a place called Massanbuany. None of his maps showed it so he took a drive up the coast and finally found it.

He walked into the government building, recalling that the angel had said things would happen in the government to bring revival that would spread throughout many parts of Africa. In that building was a man with a big smile to greet him. The man said, "Morris Plotts! You are famous in our country! I am the district official over 110,000 people. I am a Christian! I was just promoted, which is strange because I have never been promoted before. There are a lot of Muslims in this area. But now everything seems to be going right."

They started comparing dates, and it was the date that that angel was on an assignment in Massanbuany, Kenya that everything started working out for this Christian official. He said, "Reverend Plotts, would you please come over to our house for dinner, and you must meet my wife."

People started hungering for the Word of God in that area. Morris got New Testaments in Swahili and gave one to each of the 110,000 people under the rulership of this Christian district official, and 10,000 Muslims gave their lives to Jesus; a great revival broke out and they pinpointed that it was the beginning of the revival that is still going on today south of the Sahara. Church growth researchers said even now 16,000 people a day are coming to Christ!

That revival began when a harvesting angel carried out a God-given assignment.

God loves you so much that He sends angels to watch over you, protect you, surround your family and your property — and even chase and persecute your enemies!

Chapter 10

Angels, Wealth And Persecution

■ *The fifth thing angels do is gather wealth for us.*

In First Kings 19:5, Elijah was given a hot meal by an angel. In David's day, God caused wealth to pour in from all over the world for the construction of the temple (and I am sure angels were part of the effort).

Pastor John Weaver, an unpretentious, humble pastor in Bozeman, Montana had a debt on his church from the previous pastor, and it was a burden to him. One day he was tracking elk in the woods and from a distance he saw a man coming. John had a warm feeling inside, and the man said, "Do you know who I am?" John said, "I believe you are an angel from God." The man said, "Yes, that is right. The Lord sent me here. What is it that you want?" John said, "I would like to get the church paid off." The angel said, "I will take care of it for you," then walked behind a bush and disappeared.

The very next morning, somebody came to the pastor's office and gave him a check for half the amount of the church's debt, with a promise to pay the rest off in a short time. Soon the church was debt-free.

I have read surveys that show that tithing Christians earn an average of $20,000 more than non-tithing Christians. That is because angels touch what they have and it goes farther and it lasts longer!

■　　*Number six: Angels persecute the ungodly.*

> May they be like chaff before the wind, with the angel of the LORD driving them away; may their path be dark and slippery, with the angel of the LORD pursuing them.
>
> —Psalm 35:5-6

God loves you so much that He sends angels to watch over you, protect you, surround your family and your property — and even chase and persecute your enemies!

> God is just: He will pay back trouble to those who trouble you and give relief to you who are troubled, and to us as well. This will happen when the Lord Jesus is revealed from heaven in blazing fire with his powerful angels.
>
> —2 Thessalonians 1:6-7

Angels play a key role in persecuting people who trouble believers. They chase, pursue, harm, and harass them. Think about those folks who have troubled you with ridicule, gossip, and backbiting. Can you picture an angel walking beside them giving them constant problems, tripping them up, spoiling their plans? It happens! Remember, God said that vengeance belongs to Him, and He carries out that vengeance in part by sending angels to persecute the ungodly.

In the book of Acts, an angel struck down Herod for accepting praise from the people.

> Immediately, because Herod did not give praise to God, an angel of the Lord struck him down, and he was eaten by worms and died.
>
> —Acts 12:23

In the Old Testament, God sent an angel to do away with Israel's enemies.

> For I will defend this city, to save it, for mine own sake, and for my servant David's sake. And it came to pass that night, that the angel of the LORD went out, and smote in the camp of the Assyrians an hundred fourscore and five thousand: and when they arose early in the morning, behold, they *were* all dead corpses.
>
> —2 Kings 19:34-35 (KJV)

Nowadays we don't see angels killing thousands of people all at once like that — or do we? Is it possible that angels have much more to do with world events than we might suspect? That is a question only God can answer, but it is still true that some angels are sent to earth simply to harass our enemies, and thank God for that.

Have you ever known somebody who seems to have one problem after another? Could there be an angel involved? Perhaps God is troubling him because he troubles others.

■   *Number seven: Sing, worship, and rejoice.*

> But you have come to Mount Zion, to the heavenly Jerusalem, the city of the living God. You have come to thousands upon thousands of angels in joyful assembly.
>
> —Hebrews 12:22

One of the most well-known functions of angels is to sing, worship, and rejoice. We see this in Luke chapter two, when the angels appeared to shepherds in the field to announce the birth of Jesus, they praised God saying, "Glory to God in the highest, and on earth, peace to men on whom His favor rests."

> Praise him, all his angels, praise him, all his heavenly hosts.
>
> —Psalm 148:2

> And again, when God brings his firstborn into the world, he says, "Let all God's angels worship him."
>
> —Hebrews 1:6

In the book of Revelation we get numerous glimpses of the heavens full of worshiping angels. They fall on their faces before the throne and ascribe all glory, majesty and power to the Father (Revelation 4).

In fact, some scholars believe that Lucifer was in charge of leading praise and worship before he fell. That may or may not be true — the Bible does not explicitly say — but we do know that there are four classes of angels. The ministering angels are under the direction of the Holy Spirit Himself; the warring angels are under the direction of Michael; and the messenger angels are under the direction of Gabriel. But the Bible does not say who leads the worshiping angels. That is why some people say that Satan, when he was still a faithful angel, was in charge of the music in Heaven.

Whether or not that is true, I am sure that he despises worship directed toward God. I was in a service one time listening to another man preach, and as we worshiped at one point people began to sing in the Spirit. It was beautiful and heavenly. I believe that when people sing in the Spirit they are sometimes singing in the language of angels. Paul said:

> **Though I speak with the tongues of men *and of angels*...**
>
> **—1 Corinthians 13:1 (KJV, italics added)**

Angels have a language! We can praise God in the tongues of men — English, Spanish, French, German — but we can also praise Him in the language of angels, which we don't presently understand but which is directed by the Spirit.

On one occasion, something even more unusual happened at a service I attended. As we were singing in the Spirit, suddenly, as if from the ceiling — it was hard to identify where it was coming from — other voices joined in. It was like my ears could suddenly hear more than they ever had before and I could hear into the realm of the Spirit. They were the most beautiful voices I have ever heard in my life, and they were singing. I thought, "Am I dying? Am I going to Heaven?" Then someone else said, "I hear angels singing." And the preacher said, "The choirs of Heaven have joined with us in worshiping Jesus." I believe on that one occasion — and only then, in all my years of being a Christian — I listened in on the choirs of Heaven.

Angels also rejoice when sinners come into the family of God.

> In the same way, I tell you, there is rejoicing in the presence of the angels of God over one sinner who repents.
>
> —Luke 15:10

Why do they rejoice? Because they do not want to carry out judgment and persecution! They would much rather that people turn to God than suffer.

Joe was a Jew who was saved in 1967. First Corinthians says that Jews require a sign, and to this day it is still true. Joe was unsure of whether he was making the right decision. Friends took him to be baptized at a river and they prayed secretly, "Lord, we know that Joe is still uneasy, so please give Joe a sign that this is Your plan and Your will."

Joe waded into the water and the preacher prepared to baptize him. Just as he was going under the water, singing voices came out of the sky, voices that nobody in the group could identify. They realized that angels had joined in. Joe got his sign: the angels were rejoicing.

Angels don't always look like angels.

Chapter 11

Angels That Look Like Us

■ *Number eight almost goes without saying: Angels deliver answers to prayer.*

In Acts 12:1-12 Peter was rescued from jail and execution by an angel — after the church prayed. In Daniel 9:20-23, Gabriel the angel came to Daniel and said he had been dispatched from Heaven the moment Daniel started praying.

I was reading a book by George Otis and he told a story about a man named Norman who was traveling to the Canary Islands. That morning his mother prayed with him saying, "Father, I feel pressed to ask you to surround Norman with angels. Protect him wherever he goes."

It was a foggy afternoon and the flight was to leave at 5 p.m. The Pan American 747 received clearance from the tower to taxi down the runway. It was supposed to turn left on taxiway "C," then turn right and come around to face the runway, but sitting at the end of the runway was a Dutch KLM 747, and as Captain Grubb turned his Pan American 747 to backtaxi down the runway he noticed the take-off lights of the KLM jet that had started its unauthorized roll down the runway for take-off.

The Pan American 747 was going one way, the KLM jet was going the other. People began to scream as Norman and the others saw the KLM plane coming. Captain Grubb gave his jet full throttle and turned it off the runway and onto the grass to try to avoid a crash. The captain of the KLM realized that the Pan American plane was on the runway and tried to pull his jet off the ground before it was up to speed, but it hit the top section of the Pan American 747. The KLM burst into flames, and the people aboard it disintegrated.

Captain Grubb tried to get as many people out of his jet as he could, but the plane was heaving, exploding, fire was everywhere, and the air was filled with moans, groans and cries for loved ones. Some people were burning to death in their seats.

Norman stood up and screamed, "In the name of Jesus Christ and by Your shed blood, though I walk through the fire, I shall not be burned!" Immediately, something picked him up and moved him. Flames burst through the floor where he was just standing. He said it again, "In the name of Jesus Christ and by Your shed blood, though I walk through the fire, I shall not be burned!"

Something picked him up and moved him again! All around, he could see people exploding as if by spontaneous combustion. He could hear the cries and smell the burning flesh, and he kept saying, "In the name of Jesus Christ and by Your shed blood, though I walk through the fire, I shall not be burned!"

Now he was up to the front part of the plane. There was a hole blown through the top of the double-decker aircraft, but no way for Norman to get to it. It was his only chance at survival. He said, "God, help me," and when he opened his eyes, he was on top of the airplane sliding down onto the wing. He jumped to the ground and ran to safety.

Something carried him through that burning plane. Something lifted him through that hole in the roof. Something protected him as he jumped off the wing of that airplane and ran to safety. Angels had been dispatched by God to answer his prayers.

The Wicked City

Angels work cooperatively with us in intercessory prayer, too. They answer our prayers when we pray on behalf of others. Abraham learned this when God told him He was going to destroy Sodom and Gomorrah (Genesis 19). Abraham's nephew, Lot, had moved there and raised a family. Abraham said to the Lord, "My nephew's family is there. Is there any way to save them before the cities are destroyed?" He began interceding, and because of his intercessory prayer two angels went into Sodom, grabbed Lot, his wife, two of his daughters, and ran out of town just before the burning sulfur came down.

Angels still do that today. When we pray, God dispatches them to deliver instant answers.

■ *Number nine: Angels manifest as humans.*

Angels don't always look like angels. We learned earlier how they can show up for dinner in disguise. Obviously, if an angel were to come into our house in his full glory we would, at the very least, be overwhelmed, and would quite likely faint because of the intensity of God's glory on them.

What do angels normally look like? Sometimes in the Bible they appear in their splendor as ministers of fire, shrouded in flames, glowing like bronze, and giving off blinding light. The prophet Daniel was dumbstruck when an angel came to him in its heavenly brilliance. Ezekiel lost all power to stand. John the apostle fell down repeatedly as his body gave way under the incredible power of God's presence.

But oftentimes, angels appear just like human beings. When that happens, we are tempted to doubt that we are really seeing an angel. We think, "Maybe there is a trap door and he walked down the steps." That is why people who have angel experiences can still backslide like anybody else. A supernatural experience is never enough to make us faithful.

My friend, Ken Gaub, an evangelist from Yakima, Washington, flew into Seattle one night and began the hundred and fifty mile drive across the mountains to Yakima. At the summit of the pass, he pulled over at a little convenience store to get some coffee, but the place was closed. When he got back into his van, it wouldn't start. No one was around and it was pitch black. There was nothing open nearby. Ken realized he didn't have many options, so he decided to sleep in the van until morning and then fix the problem.

As he was laying there, he woke up as another vehicle, a battered small car, backed in beside the van. The driver motioned for him to roll his window down. Even though he thought this might be some weirdo wanting to cause harm, he complied. The man said, "Van won't start, huh?"

Ken said, "No."

The stranger continued, "A bolt has fallen out of your starter. If you tighten up the other bolt, it will get you home." He paused, "You want me to fix it?"

Ken was extremely surprised by this diagnosis. He countered, "You think you can?"

The man replied, "Sure."

He got out of his car carrying a socket wrench with a long handle and a piece of blue bubble wrap, walked around to the passenger side, laid down on the bubble wrap, and slid under the van. He began to work in complete darkness. In a few minutes, he slid back out and said, "Okay, it'll start now."

Ken turned the key, and the van started right up. He got out of the van and reached into his pocket, saying, "Thank You! Here, let me pay you."

The stranger looked at the money, laughed, and asked, "What would I do with money?"

Ken said, "I'm from Yakima."

The man replied, "Yes, I know."

Ken asked, "Where are you from?"

He replied, "Heaven."

Ken put the money away, got back into the van and drove on to Yakima, thanking God for sending him an angel to help him get home. He no longer needed that cup of coffee.

Two Mothers?

A mother who had a straw farm for making straw brooms was out picking straw with her four-year-old son and the straw was way over his head. He wandered off and got far away from his mother. He called her name but there was no answer. Finally he cried out, "Jesus, help me." Just then, his mother (he thought) gently took his hand and said, "Come on, son, let's go back to the house."

He and his "mother" walked back to the house, and when they got to the back porch, the door opened and his mother said, "I have been looking all over for you." The boy looked behind him, and the other mother was gone! His real mother said, "I thought you came back to the house, so I came looking for you. I have been so worried!" He said, "I was lost until you came and got me." She said, "I did not come and get you." Then he realized, in child-like understanding, that an angel appeared in human form as his mother and had taken him home.

An Angelic House Cleaner

My friend Loren Triplett tells a wonderful, true story about an angel that helped his mother when he was a young man. The Triplett family was living temporarily in a small city in Oregon where Loren's father was speaking as an evangelist for a few months. The Tripletts had five children, and one day Gladys was absolutely exhausted from taking care of the house and the children. She had barely slept for five nights. The house was a mess; laundry was piled up; the dishes were not done. Her husband was off to morning prayer meetings at the church where he was preaching, and she in her desperation got on her knees and said, "God, I cannot go on. I need some rest. Please help me."

At ten thirty in the morning, there came a knock at the door, and there was a lady with a scarf over her head. Gladys thought she had come for prayer and was not about to turn her away, but the lady said, "No, my dear child. You have misunderstood. I have not come for prayer. I have come as an answer to your prayer. You called out to the Father for help. I am here now."

Gladys sat down. She was intrigued by the woman. There was a strangeness about her, but at the same time a warm peace. Her scarf and clothes were wet from the rain and she said, "Do you mind if I use the bathroom to dry off?"

She walked into the bathroom and thirty seconds later walked out totally dry. She looked at Gladys and said, "Honey, you need some rest. Let's put you on the couch and cover you up. The Father knows you need it." She picked up Gladys, laid her on the couch and pulled a little blanket over her. Instantly Gladys fell asleep.

Three hours later she woke up. She felt like she had slept for days, she was so refreshed. She looked around and all the laundry was done, folded, fluffed and put in the drawers. It would have taken two days to do all the laundry because she did not have a dryer. The table was set for thirteen people; the kitchen was spotlessly clean, and there was dinner cooking in the oven. The baby had been bathed and changed.

Gladys approached the woman and said, "What is your name?" The woman said, "Dear, just say I am a servant of the Lord." Gladys said, "Why did you set the table for thirteen? There are only seven of us." The woman said, "You are going to be having guests for dinner tonight." Just then, Reverend Triplett came home, and a carload of people with him. Somebody in the church had died and so they canceled the morning meetings and brought people home for lunch.

There were exactly thirteen. Gladys did not know where this woman got the groceries. It was the most wonderful meal that they had ever had in that little parsonage.

After dinner the lady said, "You rest. I will clean up." She took all the dirty dishes into the kitchen. A few minutes later, she walked out and said, "Everything's cleaned up." Gladys went into the kitchen and everything was washed, dried and put away! She said, "I must be going now, child," and she left. Everybody said good-bye to her.

Gladys and her husband thought they should thank her, so they searched all over the small town for the mystery woman. They described the woman, the way she talked, the way she looked, what she wore, but nobody had ever heard of such a woman. The Tripletts even went to the police department to try to track her down, but they never found her.

That story reminds me of Peter's experience when an angel delivered him from jail.

> ...the angel departed from him. And when Peter was come to himself, he said, Now I know of a surety, that the Lord hath sent his angel, and hath delivered me out of the hand of Herod, and *from* all the expectation of the people of the Jews.
>
> —Acts 12:10-11 (KJV)

Like Gladys Triplett, Peter only realized he had an angel encounter after the angel was gone.

Chapter 12

Ministering To Believers

The tenth thing angels do is minister to believ-
ers in times of spiritual need.

> Are not all angels ministering spirits sent to
> serve those who will inherit salvation?
>
> —Hebrews 1:14

Angels don't just rescue us from physical danger
— they bring spiritual refreshing straight from God.
We see this in Jesus' life. The night before He was to
be crucified.

> He withdrew about a stone's throw beyond
> them, knelt down and prayed, "Father, if you
> are willing, take this cup from me; yet not my
> will, but yours be done." An angel from heaven
> appeared to him and strengthened him.
>
> —Luke 22:41-43

Earlier in His life, when He was being tempted in
the desert, angels were there.

> Jesus said to him, "Away from me, Satan! For it is written: `Worship the Lord your God, and serve him only.'" Then the devil left him, and angels came and attended him.

> —Matthew 4:10-11

When we find ourselves hard-pressed, weak, or spiritually dry God will often send angels to us. God sent angels to Hagar when she ran away into the desert (see Genesis 16:7), and again when she thought her son Ishmael would die.

> God heard the boy crying, and the angel of God called to Hagar from heaven and said to her, "What is the matter, Hagar? Do not be afraid; God has heard the boy crying as he lies there."

> —Genesis 21:17

Angels can chase away our doubts and fears. A woman named Nancy was terrified of flying, but something came up in her family that required her and her husband to take a plane. She was so scared that when they boarded she felt pains in her chest; her hands were white as a sheet of paper. She gripped the handles on the seats and said, "Jesus, help me."

She looked out the window, and there was an angel sitting on the wing of the airplane looking in at her. Nancy said, "Look! Look!" but nobody else could see him. She felt great comfort knowing that God sent an angel and allowed her to see him. Every now and then the angel would look in at Nancy and smile, and when the plane was coming in for a landing, just a few feet off the ground, the angel looked at her and smiled — almost to say, "My mission's accomplished." He shot straight up in the air, the plane landed safely and Nancy has not been afraid of flying since. God gave her a heavenly vision for that special time to help her overcome her fears.

In The Volume Of The Book

A pastor I know was going through some difficult situations in his church. He was praying, crying out to God, and went to the church. Just then, he looked up at the back of the church and through a window, a light began to come toward him, and it got bigger and brighter, and in that light was a man holding a book. He could not see his face but this figure said to him, "Lo, in the volume of the book it is written." He no sooner said it than he began to fade away through the same window.

This pastor recognized the words as being from Psalm 40 and Hebrews 10, and so he got his Bible and looked up Psalm 40:7 (KJV) where it says, "Lo, I come: in the volume of the book it is written of me," and by reading it in context he found answers to all the questions he had about his situation.

My Own Experience

I believe I met an angel one time. I was experiencing a great deal of anguish about the way things were going in the church. Certain groups of people were promoting rebellion and subversiveness and I did not know how to deal with them without causing serious repercussions and alienating other people in the church. I was in utter turmoil and did not know what to do. I had mustered all the faith I could, but it did not seem to be working, and I was ready to throw in the towel. I was at a low point that not many people knew about.

I boarded an airplane in St. Louis, Missouri, heading for Tulsa. They gave me a seat in the DC-9 on the side of the plane with two seats, and the seat next to me was still empty after everybody got on board. I thought, "Great. I am going to stretch out." Then I saw a tall man walk onto the plane very slowly and something warm came over me. Usually I like having room to stretch, but this time I was hoping this man would sit next to me. He was radiant. As he approached he looked right at me, and his eye caught mine. I don't normally think things like this but I immediately thought, "I wonder if he is an angel."

He looked at me and jokingly said, "I hate flying this way."

"This way?" What did he mean when he said, "I hate flying *this way*?" Was he giving me a clue as to his true origin?

I was speechless. Every time he looked at me an indescribable warmth came over me. I gathered enough courage to say, "Where are you going?"

He said, "I just finished up my assignment in St. Louis, and now I am on another assignment."

He looked at me, and did not say a word, but suddenly there was communication between us. I will grant that I was under a lot of stress that day and may have been hearing things in my mind, but I don't think I was making it up. He did not say a word verbally, but he started "telling" me about the people that were causing me the greatest stress, about the deep pain in their lives, the hurt they have experienced. All of a sudden I had love for the people I had been hating, and I felt overwhelmed with the desire to intercede for them.

He told me things about my life, about other peoples' lives that I needed to know, and as this communication was going on I felt bathed in love. Then I thought, "I better write this stuff down," and I began to take notes, several pages worth. If it was a human being next to me, not an angel like I suspect it was, he probably thought I was a nut because I was scribbling so furiously. When I was done writing he told me to seal it up because many of the things were not to be revealed yet.

As the airplane approached Tulsa the wind was out of the north, a rare occurrence for that city, and so we had to approach from the south. I have flown into Tulsa dozens of times and never approached from the south. But there was a reason.

I looked out the window, and there below us was Oral Roberts University. The man sitting next to me pointed out the window, and said verbally, "That is Oral Roberts University." Suddenly there were no more words, but the communication began again and he started telling me things about Oral and Evelyn Roberts, about the hurts and the pain that their family has experienced over the years and how most of that pain has come from people in the body of Christ. I understood things about Oral Roberts that I did not understand before, and I had so much love for Oral and Evelyn. The angel told me, "You have heard Oral Roberts say that everybody is sick in some way. Everybody would be kinder to each other if they knew how everybody hurts in some way."

We landed and my mind was still reeling from the experience. I got off the airplane and decided to wait and watch the man get off. One after another, people emerged from the jetway but not him. When the plane was totally empty, I went down to the baggage claim, but he was not there, and I never saw him again.

Did I have an angel experience? I cannot say for sure, but I felt ministered to in a way that has seldom happened to me. Those precious few moments on the airplane changed my life.

Not all messages from Heaven are the ones people want to receive.

Chapter 13

Bad News Angels

■ *The eleventh thing angels do is carry believers to Heaven.*

They do not simply escort them; they actually carry them, becoming the means of transportation for believers who die and go to be with Jesus. Luke 16:22 tells about this in the parable of the rich man and Lazarus.

As a pastor, I have been with Christians who were on death's door. Virtually every time, they said they saw angels arrive. One lady said, "The angels are here now." She smiled, closed her eyes and left.

That will happen to each of us someday. At the moment our hearts stop beating, we will be carried by angels into the presence of Jesus. I believe we will find great comfort in that.

■ *Number twelve: Angels bring supernatural provision.*

Angels brought food to Elijah which gave him enough energy to last for weeks. Can you imagine just eating one meal every ten days? That's all you would need if it was angel food.

In Genesis 21:16-19, an angel showed Hagar and her son where to find water, sparing them from death. I believe angels still bring supernatural provision, though we can't always see them.

■ *Number thirteen: Angels bring bad news to people in rebellion.*

Not all messages from Heaven are the ones people want to receive. There are judgment angels and they are not benign, cupid-type creatures. They are tough, strong, powerful, mighty beings to carry out the judgment of God.

• During the time of the Exodus a destroying angel took the lives of the firstborns of the Egyptians.

• In Acts 12:23, an "angel of the Lord" struck Herod dead, as we saw earlier.

• In Revelation 8:10-11, an angel poisons the water during the time of tribulation.

• In 1 Corinthians 10:10 Paul tells about those who were destroyed by the destroying angel because of the sins of their tongue.

• In Judges 5:23 (KJV) a song was sung about the angel who cried:

> **Curse ye Meroz, said the angel of the LORD, curse ye bitterly the inhabitants thereof; because they came not to the help of the LORD, to the help of the LORD against the mighty.**

These are not harmless do-gooders. They are judgment angels with severe missions to carry out.

Angels also bring warnings of danger. These come not to deliver judgment but to help people avoid it.

An angel came to Joseph and said, "Herod is going to search for the child to kill him. Leave and go to Egypt." Joseph listened to the angel, took Jesus and Mary and fled to Egypt. Sure enough, Herod had every baby two years old and younger murdered. Jesus was spared because Joseph took heed of the angel's words.

Paul was in a hopeless situation one time. It is recorded in Acts 27. He was on a ship that never should have sailed. There was a storm coming; the captain knew it but decided to press on. When you have a certain degree of expertise you get cocky and think you can beat it. That is why so many airplane pilots get into trouble. After you have flown for a while and have been in a few storms you tend to think, "That is no big deal. I've gone through worse." Yet a lot of the aviation accidents are the result of flying into bad weather.

The ship ran into a hurricane. The crew knew they were going to sink, so they tried fasting. Paul went down to sleep, and he opened his eyes and there was a silhouette and a light — an angel there to give him a word of comfort and warning. He said, "Paul, you are right. This ship is going to be wrecked, but every life will be spared."

Paul got up and said, "Break the fast, start eating. The angel of the Lord came to me last night and told me that yes, we are going to be shipwrecked but every life will be spared." And sure enough, when the ship wrecked there were enough pieces of wood for people to float on and everybody was spared.

That's the kind of warning we all want to receive — one that tells us everything will work out, even through the hard times.

What if you encounter an angel? What if you, like Paul, go into your bedroom to sleep and find yourself face to face with an angel? Is it possible to be ready if such a thing happens? In the next chapter we will find out.

Chapter 14

What To Do If You Meet An Angel

While I was preaching one day, I felt an unusual anointing of God's presence and power, and after the service several people came up to me — people who were stable and I knew to be spiritual — and said, "Pastor Williams, when you were preaching, it was like a great curtain was lifted between time and eternity, and I saw two angels beside you. One was on the right side and one was on the left side, and when you would walk, they would walk right with you."

Others have told me that at times God allows them to see into the spirit and they see me surrounded by angels.

I have never seen the angels around me that others see, and I don't feel the need to. I am comforted knowing they are there. Sometime God may allow you to peer through to the other side to encourage you, to show you the protection around you or around someone you love. At other times an angel may come to you in the appearance of a person and you will not know it is an angel.

But perhaps someday you will have a face-to-face experience with an angel that causes you to tremble. I am expecting more angelic involvement as we get closer to the return of Jesus, and it would not surprise me to hear of more Christians being visited by angels, just as the believers in the Early Church were.

If it happens, what should you do? I have gleaned these points from the Bible. Maybe someday you will be in a position to use them.

■   *Be respectful.*

Remember that angels live in perfection with God. Also remember that they only come to us on God's direct word. We need to treat them with the utmost respect as fellow servants of the Most High.

Peter recognized this when he wrote:

> This is especially true of those who follow the corrupt desire of the sinful nature and despise authority. Bold and arrogant, these men are not afraid to slander celestial beings; yet even angels, although they are stronger and more pow-

erful, do not bring slanderous accusations
against such beings in the presence of the Lord.

—2 Peter 2:10-11

That means that there is a code of conduct in the
spiritual realm that we dare not violate. If the Bible
tells us not to even slander demons, how much more
should we offer respect to faithful messengers of God.

■ *Don't worship them.*

As we have seen, angels refuse to be worshiped.
You may be tempted by the brilliance and majesty
emanating from them, but do not bow down and worship them.

■ *Don't focus on the angel but on God.*

Remember that God is vastly more powerful and
loving than the angel that is before you. The angel is
simply a servant. He cannot answer your prayer and
can only act within the measure of authority God has
given him.

■ *Test what the angel says by the Bible.*

No matter how impressed you might be by the
appearance of an angel, make sure his words or in-
structions line up with the Bible. Do not accept any
message, exhortation, or instruction that is out of line
with the Bible.

Obey And Don't Doubt!

If an angel's words are clearly from God, obey and do not be skeptical. Learn from the experience of Zechariah, father of John the Baptist, who doubted Gabriel's words and was struck mute until John was born. Be instead like Mary, mother of Jesus, who humbly received Gabriel's words with faith.

If you do not obey or receive the word, you expose yourself to great danger. The writer of Hebrews said:

> We must pay more careful attention, therefore, to what we have heard, so that we do not drift away. For if the message spoken by angels was binding, and every violation and disobedience received its just punishment, how shall we escape if we ignore such a great salvation?
>
> —Hebrews 2:1-3a

Don't try to contact the angel once he's gone.

We can have a deep respect for angels, but we are not to try to cultivate friendships or acquaintances with them. As a matter of fact, we are not even allowed to talk to angels unless they talk or appear to us first.

When Samson's parents were visited by an angel they probably yearned to see him again, but they did not try to contact him. In fact, they knew it was an angel from God because he did not return:

So Manoah took a kid with a meat offering, and offered *it* upon a rock unto the LORD: and *the angel* did wondrously; and Manoah and his wife looked on. For it came to pass, when the flame went up toward heaven from off the altar, that the angel of the LORD ascended in the flame of the altar. And Manoah and his wife looked on *it,* and fell on their faces to the ground. But the angel of the LORD did no more appear to Manoah and to his wife. *Then Manoah knew that he was an angel of the LORD.*

—Judges 13:19-21 (KJV, italics added)

As a Christian, angels are surrounding you and doing so much to ensure your success and well-being.

The Last Word

I hear more and more reports from credible ministries and people about angelic visitors from another realm. It seems to me that there have been more and more angel sightings, and the angels almost always warn of impending judgment and point to the Lord Jesus Christ.

Angels are wonderful partners in the work of God. They:

- protect us.

- deliver messages to us.

- visit with us in human disguise.

- bring people to Christ.

- gather wealth for us.

- persecute the ungodly.

- sing, worship and rejoice.

- deliver answers to prayer.

- minister to believers' spiritual needs.

- bring supernatural provision.

- carry believers to Heaven when they die.

There are probably thousands of other things angels do, too, but this is what we know from the Bible.

I hope you feel encouraged knowing that, as a Christian, angels are surrounding you and doing so much to ensure your success and well-being. I hope you have more confidence distinguishing good angels from bad angels, and seeing through the confusion that so often goes along with discussions of angels. I also hope you have an idea what to do if you are ever visited by an angel.

Whether or not we see angels in this life is not important. One day we will be with them around the throne of God, and there will be no more mystery. The important thing to remember is that we are all here — angels and humans — to serve God, and for His glorious purposes on earth.

About The Author

Dave Williams is pastor of Mount Hope Church and International Outreach Ministries, with world headquarters in Lansing, Michigan. He has served for over 20 years, leading the church in Lansing from 226 to over 4000 today. Dave sends trained ministers into unreached cities to establish disciple-making churches, and, as a result, today has "branch" churches in the United States, Philippines, and in Africa.

Dave is the founder and president of Mount Hope Bible Training Institute, a fully accredited institute for training ministers and lay people for the work of the ministry. He has authored 45 books including the fifteen-time best seller, *The Start of Something Wonderful* (with over 2,000,000 books sold), and more recently, *The Miracle Results of Fasting*, and *The Road To Radical Riches*.

The Pacesetter's Path telecast is Dave's weekly television program seen over a syndicated network of secular stations, and nationally over the Sky Angel satellite system. Dave has produced over 125 audio cassette programs including the nationally acclaimed *School of Pacesetting Leadership* which is being used as a training program in churches around the United States, and in Bible Schools in South Africa and the Philippines. He is a popular speaker at conferences, seminars, and conventions. His speaking ministry has taken him across America, Africa, Europe, Asia, and other parts of the world.

Along with his wife, Mary Jo, Dave established The Dave and Mary Jo Williams Charitable Mission (Strategic Global Mission), a mission's ministry for providing scholarships to pioneer pastors and grants to inner-city children's ministries.

Dave's articles and reviews have appeared in national magazines such as *Advance, The Pentecostal Evangel, Ministries Today, The Lansing Magazine, The Detroit Free Press* and others. Dave, as a private pilot, flies for fun. He is married, has two grown children, and lives in Delta Township, Michigan.

You may write to Pastor Dave Williams:

P.O. Box 80825

Lansing, MI 48908-0825

Please include your special prayer requests when you write, or you may call the Mount Hope Global Prayer Center anytime: (517) 327-PRAY

DECAPOLIS
PUBLISHING

For a catalog of products, call:

1-517-321-2780 or

1-800-888-7284

or visit us on the web at:

www.mounthopechurch.org

For Your Spiritual Growth

Here's the help you need for your spiritual journey. These books will encourage you, and give you guidance as you seek to draw close to Jesus and learn of Him. Prepare yourself for fantastic growth!

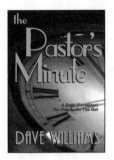

QUESTIONS I HAVE ANSWERED
Get answers to many of the questions you've always wanted to ask a pastor!

THE PASTOR'S MINUTE
A daily devotional for people on the go! Powerful topics will help you grow even when you're in a hurry.

ANGELS: THEY'RE WATCHING YOU!
The Bible tells more than you might think about these powerful beings.

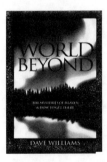

THE WORLD BEYOND
What will Heaven be like? What happens there? Will we see relatives who have gone before us? Who *REALLY* goes to Heaven?

FILLED!
Learn how you can be filled with the mightiest power in the universe. Find out what could be missing from your life.

STRATEGIC GLOBAL MISSION
Read touching stories about God's plan for accelerating the Gospel globally through reaching children and training pastors.

These and other books available from Dave Williams and:

D E C A P O L I S
P U B L I S H I N G

For Your Spiritual Growth

Here's the help you need for your spiritual journey. These books will encourage you, and give you guidance as you seek to draw close to Jesus and learn of Him. Prepare yourself for fantastic growth!

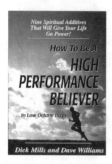

HOW TO BE A HIGH PERFORMANCE BELIEVER
Pour in the nine spiritual additives for real power in your Christian life.

SECRET OF POWER WITH GOD
Tap into the real power with God; the power of prayer. It will change your life!

THE NEW LIFE ...
You can get off to a great start on your exciting life with Jesus! Prepare for something wonderful.

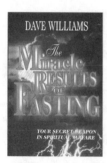

MIRACLE RESULTS OF FASTING
You can receive MIRACLE benefits, spiritually and physically, with this practical Christian discipline.

WHAT TO DO IF YOU MISS THE RAPTURE
If you miss the Rapture, there may still be hope, but you need to follow these clear survival tactics.

THE AIDS PLAGUE
Is there hope? Yes, but only Jesus can bring a total and lasting cure to AIDS.

These and other books available from Dave Williams and:

DECAPOLIS PUBLISHING

For Your Spiritual Growth

Here's the help you need for your spiritual journey. These books will encourage you, and give you guidance as you seek to draw close to Jesus and learn of Him. Prepare yourself for fantastic growth!

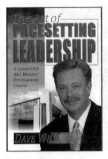

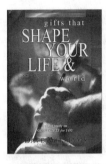

THE ART OF PACESETTING LEADERSHIP
You can become a successful leader with this proven leadership development course.

GIFTS THAT SHAPE YOUR LIFE
Learn which ministry best fits you, and discover your God-given personality gifts, as well as the gifts of others.

GROWING UP IN OUR FATHER'S FAMILY
You can have a family relationship with your heavenly father. Learn how God cares for you.

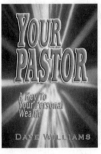

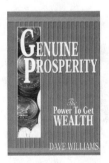

SUPERNATURAL SOULWINNING
How will we reach our family, friends, and neighbors in this short time before Christ's return?

YOUR PASTOR: A KEY TO YOUR PERSONAL WEALTH
By honoring your pastor you can actually be setting yourself up for a financial blessing from God!

GENUINE PROSPERITY
Learn what it means to be truly prosperous! God gives us the power to get wealth!

These and other books available from Dave Williams and:

DECAPOLIS PUBLISHING

For Your Spiritual Growth

Here's the help you need for your spiritual journey. These books will encourage you, and give you guidance as you seek to draw close to Jesus and learn of Him. Prepare yourself for fantastic growth!

SOMEBODY OUT THERE NEEDS YOU
Along with the gift of salvation comes the great privilege of spreading the gospel of Jesus Christ.

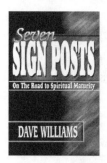

SEVEN SIGNPOSTS TO SPIRITUAL MATURITY
Examine your life to see where you are on the road to spiritual maturity.

THE PASTORS PAY
How much is your pastor worth? Who should set his pay? Discover the scriptural guidelines for paying your pastor.

DECEPTION, DELUSION & DESTRUCTION
Recognize spiritual deception and unmask spiritual blindness.

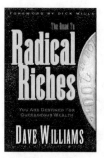

THE ROAD TO RADICAL RICHES
Are you ready to jump from "barely getting by" to Gods plan for putting you on the road to Radical Riches?

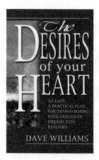

THE DESIRES OF YOUR HEART
Yes, Jesus wants to give you the desires of your heart, and make them realities.

These and other books available from Dave Williams and:

DECAPOLIS PUBLISHING

For Your Successful Life

These video cassettes will give you successful principles to apply to your whole life. Each a different topic, and each a fantastic teaching of how living by God's Word can give you total success!

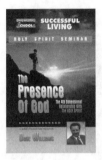

THE PRESENCE OF GOD
Find out how you can have a more dynamic relationship with the Holy Spirit.

FILLED WITH THE HOLY SPIRIT
You can rejoice and share with others in this wonderful experience of God.

GIFTS THAT CHANGE YOUR WORLD
Learn which ministry best fits you, and discover your God-given personality gifts, as well as the gifts of others.

THE SCHOOL OF PACESETTING LEADERSHIP
Leaders are made, not born. You can become a successful leader with this proven leadership development course.

MIRACLE RESULTS OF FASTING
Fasting is your secret weapon in spiritual warfare. Learn how you'll benefit spiritually and physically! Six video messages.

A SPECIAL LADY
If you feel used and abused, this video will show you how you really are in the eyes of Jesus. You are special!

These and other videos available from Dave Williams and:

For Your Successful Life

These video cassettes will give you successful principles to apply to your whole life. Each a different topic, and each a fantastic teaching of how living by God's Word can give you total success!

HOW TO BE A HIGH PERFORMANCE BELIEVER
Pour in the nine spiritual additives for real power in your Christian life.

THE UGLY WORMS OF JUDGMENT
Recognizing the decay of judgment in your life is your first step back into God's fullness.

WHAT TO DO WHEN YOU FEEL WEAK AND DEFEATED
Learn about God's plan to bring you out of defeat and into His principles of victory!

WHY SOME ARE NOT HEALED
Discover the obstacles that hold people back from receiving their miracle and how God can help them receive the very best!

BREAKING THE POWER OF POVERTY
The principality of mammon will try to keep you in poverty. Put God FIRST and watch Him bring you into a wealthy place.

HERBS FOR HEALTH
A look at the concerns and fears of modern medicine. Learn the correct ways to open the doors to your healing.

These and other videos available from Dave Williams and:

DECAPOLIS PUBLISHING

Running Your Race

These simple but powerful audio cassette singles will help give you the edge you need. Run your race to win!

LONELY IN THE MIDST OF A CROWD
Loneliness is a devastating disease. Learn how to trust and count on others to help.

HERBS FOR HEALTH
A look at the concerns and fears of modern medicine. Learn the correct ways to open the doors to your healing.

HOW TO GET ANYTHING YOU WANT
You can learn the way to get anything you want from God!

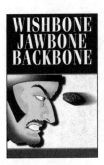

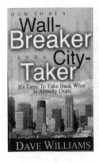

WISHBONE, JAWBONE, BACKBONE
Learn about King David, and how his three "bones" for success can help you in your life quest.

FATAL ENTICEMENTS
Learn how you can avoid the vice-like grip of sin and it's fatal enticements that hold people captive.

HOW TO BE A WALL BREAKER AND A CITY TAKER
You can be a powerful force for advancing the Kingdom of Jesus Christ!

These and other audio tapes available from Dave Williams and:

DECAPOLIS PUBLISHING

Expanding Your Faith

These exciting audio teaching series will help you to grow and mature in your walk with Christ. Get ready for amazing new adventures in faith!

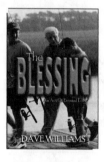

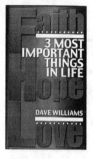

THE BLESSING
Explore the many ways that God can use you to bless others, and how He can correct the missed blessing.

SIN'S GRIP
Learn how you can avoid the vice-like grip of sin and it's fatal enticements that hold people captive.

FAITH, HOPE, & LOVE
Listen and let these three "most important things in life" change you.

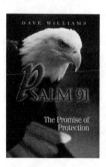

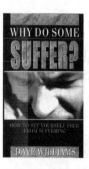

**PSALM 91
THE PROMISE OF
PROTECTION**
Everyone is looking for protection in these perilous times. God promises protection for those who rest in Him.

**DEVELOPING
THE SPIRIT OF A
CONQUEROR**
You can be a conqueror through Christ! Also, find out how to *keep* those things that you have conquered.

WHY DO SOME SUFFER
Find out why some people seem to have suffering in their lives, and find out how to avoid it in your life.

These and other audio tapes available from Dave Williams and:

DECAPOLIS
PUBLISHING

Expanding Your Faith

These exciting audio teaching series will help you to grow and mature in your walk with Christ. Get ready for amazing new adventures in faith!

ABCs OF SUCCESS AND HAPPINESS
Learn how to go after God's promises for your life. Happiness and success can be yours today!

FORGIVENESS
The miracle remedy for many of life's problems is found in this basic key for living.

UNTANGLING YOUR TROUBLES
You can be a "trouble untangler" with the help of Jesus!

HOW TO BE A HIGH PERFORMANCE BELIEVER
Put in the nine spiritual additives to help run your race and get the prize!

BEING A DISCIPLE AND MAKING DISCIPLES
You can learn to be a "disciple maker" to almost anyone.

HOW TO HELP YOUR PASTOR & CHURCH SUCCEED
You can be an integral part of your church's & pastor's success.

These and other audio tapes available from Dave Williams and:

DECAPOLIS PUBLISHING

To order this
best-selling book
by Pastor Dave Williams,
mail this form with
payment to:

THE HOPE STORE
202 South Creyts Road
Lansing, Michigan 48917-9284

or:

PHONE
517-321-2780
800-888-7284

FAX
517-321-6332

WRITE
202 S. Creyts Rd.
Lansing, MI 48917

Please enter my order as follows:

☐ NEW LIFE (English)
☐ LA NUEVA VIDA (Spanish)

2-25	_____	@1.95 ea.	_____
26-49	_____	@1.70 ea.	_____
50-99	_____	@1.50 ea.	_____
100-199	_____	@1.25 ea.	_____
200-349	_____	@1.10 ea.	_____
350-499	_____	@.95 ea.	_____
500+	_____	@.75 ea.	_____

Add 10% shipping/handling US _____
(15% shipping/handling Canada)
TOTAL INCLUDED WITH ORDER _____

Name _____

Business/Church _____

Address _____

City _____ State ____ ZIP _____

Telephone (____) _____

Mastercard ☐   Visa ☐   (see below for ordering by credit card)

Authorized Signature _____

PLEASE SEND ME: One Case (150 books) of

☐ NEW LIFE (English)   ☐ LA NUEVA VIDA (Spanish)
at the SPECIAL price of $142.50 per box **US** and $169.50 **CAN**
(plus shipping — 10% US — 15% Canada)

MAIL ALL ORDERS TO: THE HOPE STORE
202 S. Creyts Rd. Lansing, MI 48917-9284

VISA/MASTERCARD ORDERS: Call 1-800-888-7284